Pearls of
Garden Wisdom

Also by Deborah S. Tukua

Pearls of Country Wisdom
Pearls of Kitchen Wisdom

Pearls of
Garden Wisdom

Time-Saving Tips and
Techniques from a
Country Home

by Deborah S. Tukua and Vicki West

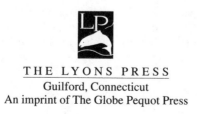

THE LYONS PRESS
Guilford, Connecticut
An imprint of The Globe Pequot Press

The Lyons Press is an imprint of The Globe Pequot Press.

Printed in the United States of America

2 4 6 8 10 9 7 5 3 1

Design by Compset, Inc.

The Library of Congress Cataloging-in-Publication Data

Tukua, Deborah, 1958–
    Pearls of garden wisdom : time-saving tips and techniques from a
country home / by Deborah S. Tukua and Vicki West.
        p. cm.
    ISBN 1-58574-401-8
    1. Gardening—Miscellanea. I. West, Vicki. II. Title.

SB453.T95 2001
635—dc21
                                                        2001038850

The tips and information in this book are intended to be a help to all who read them. They are not intended in place of professional advice. We cannot assume responsibility for any recommendations given herein. Use at your discretion please.

Dedication

And God said, Behold, I have given you every herb bearing seed, which is upon the face of all the earth, and every tree, in the which is the fruit of a tree yielding seed; to you it shall be for meat.

Genesis 1:29

This book is dedicated to all those families that garden year in and year out to feed their own families and share the bounty with others. It is to you, dear farmer, that we pay tribute with this writing in gratitude for helping supply our daily bread. The farmer, one who's not too proud to put his hands behind a plow, whose work never ceases, toils from dawn until dusk seven days a week so that we can eat and enjoy and partake of the good fruit of the earth and of the vine and of the trees. Let me express a capital thanks to you, Mr. and Mrs. Farmer U.S.A.; we appreciate all that you do for the sustaining of the life and good health of this nation. Weary not in well doing.

Deborah S. Tukua

To my precious grandson, Christian, who loves to follow Grandma in the garden. I love you Christian!

Vicki West

Contents

Acknowledgments

To the following friends and family from whom I have gleaned much about gardening and cooking fresh from the garden: Lowell Tukua, Jim Erskine, Chester Meeks, Delores Stafford, Louise Grass, Jeanne Mange, Annette Godwin, Vicki West, Sandra Curle, Cliff Millsapps, and Alan Bishop.

A continuing song of thanks to my husband and gardening partner, Lowell Tukua, for helping install new computer software; introducing me to digital cameras, gardening, and country living; tilling the soil and working out the obstacles in the way of our progress.

Thanks be to God that hung the sun, the moon and the stars, that sprouts every seed and nourishes our garden each season. Without him I am nothing.

To these precious people that graciously allowed me to photograph their fabulous lawns, gardens, and outdoor living spaces:

Tulon and Hazel Hope McRight of Florence, Alabama, for allowing me to photograph their lovely outdoor container plantings.

Jimmy L. Russ, a neighbor in the Holly Creek community of Tennessee, whose lawn and water garden is always beautifully and immaculately appointed for photographing. It's no wonder that I've seen brides in wedding gowns being photographed under his arbor on several occasions.

Faye Stooksberry, a neighbor of ours in the Holly Creek community, who decorates her lawn handsomely with nostalgic wagon wheels, birdhouses, and honeysuckle.

Becky S. Williams, owner–operator of Green Valley General Store in Bodenham, Tennessee, for allowing Dad and me to photograph her charming country store's outdoor displays.

Phyllis Stricklin, owner–operator of Main Street Treasures in Waynesboro, Tennessee, for welcoming me to photograph her adorable garden shed and outdoor container plantings.

Jo Parkhurst, curator of Pope's Tavern and Museum in Florence, Alabama, for allowing the herb wheel garden designed and maintained by the local garden clubs to be photographed.

Bob and Barbara Wilkins of Pleasantville, Tennessee, for permitting me to photograph their beehives and raised garden beds.

And to Amy Grass and Josiah Tukua, my gardening buddy and favorite fieldhand, for posing so nicely. Gardening is most enjoyable with you at my side, Josiah.

To my faithful father, Ray Stafford, a photographer trying to retire, but giving in to the requests of his daughter and admirer, who just can't let his talents go to waste. Thanks, Dad, for working with me on the photographs for this undertaking. I won't forget your willingness to help.

To Janet Perry, for enthusiastically taking photographs of us outdoors on a cold winter's day and in spring trying to overcome the prevailing high-noon shadow.

To Becky Koh, my editor, who is such a pleasure to continue to work with and from whom I am learning much.

To Vicki West, for pairing up with me on this project. It's been fun and sheer joy working with you, my friend. Let's do it again.

Deborah S. Tukua

My gratefulness, praise and honor to the wonderful Creator. I'd like to express my appreciation to Deborah Tukua who gave me the opportunity to co-author this book. It has been a true joy—an inspiration to work with you, Deborah!

To my husband, Tim, who was behind me in the writing of this book. Thank you for keeping the fires going in the greenhouse, breaking ground in the garden, and bringing home plenty of straw and hay. What a blessing, Jasmine, Cecilia, and Hannah, who bring such sweet harmony when helping in the garden. I love you girls!

To my dear Mom, who taught me how to stuff squash blossoms. Thanks for allowing me to make all kinds of dirt messes on the porch, in the yard, and in the house when I was growing up.

To Mike, for always being informative and supportive of most of my endeavors—remember growing tomatoes in "concrete"?

To my son Rick and his sweet wife, Michelle, and my grandson, Christian.

Thank you so much, Janet Perry, for your never-ceasing excitement and encouragement and for taking great pictures. Special thanks to our friends and neighbors in the Cane Creek and Russell Creek communities for their patient example in teaching and sharing garden and farming knowledge and a wonderful way of life. To my friends: Mrs. Betty Tucker, the Lobelville Library, Lean Najera, "Snooks" Moore, Erin Otto, Nancy and Romey Prince, Betty Fielder, Annette Godwin, Louise Grass, Eva Gentry, Catherine and Woody Woodpecker, Kevin and Teresa, Ralph and Blake, Larry and Nancy Hendrix, Joe and Cathy Vick, and to the many friends and customers that visited our home, gardens, and little store—thank you all.

Vicki West

❧ *Note* ❧

The cornucopia of advice shared in the following chapters has been gathered from experienced gardeners—our neighbors and friends. As with any neighborly advice, some is based on techniques and some on tradition. Select the tips, advice, and projects suitable to your gardening needs, keeping in mind that what works for one may not turn out the same for another due to varying conditions of climate, soil, etc. Above all, enjoy your time in the soil; successful gardening help is at hand in bountiful proportions.

Introduction

Although man's survival has been dependent on the fruit of the soil since his days in the first garden, it is still a miracle to witness every sprouting plant break through the seed and push up new green growth through the darkness of the soil, reaching always toward the sun. With each garden we excitedly examine the tender plants for flowering blooms and count the number of young zucchini, cucumber, and squash growing. After a good rain, we stand in wonder, amazed as to how that zucchini or cucumber could grow so fast! Why, it hadn't been but a day or so ago that it was but a mere hint on the vine. It was almost as though it grew before our very eyes.

Gardening reminds us of our dependency on God. In excellent conditions, with just the right amount of water and sunlight, our garden flourishes and at harvest we consider ourselves blessed. We offer thanks before we partake of the bounty, humbly acknowledging the fact that we are again receiving our portion from our Merciful Maker.

Gardening illustrates the life cycle of all living creatures and serves as a reminder of the brevity of our own life. Time passes and our children seem to mature and grow as quickly as the fruit ripens on the vine. We must nurture and encourage growth and care for the loved ones so entrusted to us or they will wither on the vine as a garden suffers in a drought. The environment into which we place our budding babies and the things to which we expose them greatly affect and influence their physical health and spiritual well-being. Farm life and gardening not only provides a healthy environment for our loved ones; it gives many parallels to ponder with regard to the relationships we treasure. A garden yields food for the flesh and much food for thought!

It is our desire that this book will enhance your gardening knowledge and skills, yielding hours of satisfaction in the soil as you pursue man's oldest and most popular pastime.

Happy Harvesting,
DST and VW

General Gardening Tips

We moved from our old farm to our new farm in the middle of a scorching hot July. Along with packing, hauling, then unpacking, there was a tremendous amount of work to be done. Vegetables were waiting to be harvested and preserved. For a while we were taking care of the plants and animals simultaneously at both farms, as they were just a few miles apart. It seems we spent weeks just picking, planting, canning, moving, mulching, drying, and trying to keep from crying.

The herb garden at the old farm had been growing with us for years and I just didn't have the heart to leave all those beautiful plants behind. After we'd been together so long it just wouldn't seem right not to take them with us. Even though it was the middle of the summer, my three daughters and I made up our minds to transplant what we could. Transplanting in the hottest time of the year was a bit tricky. When I told some of my gardener friends what we planned to do, most just shook their heads and asked, "Why don't you just plant seeds in the spring?" I just smiled and said, "We'll try transplanting. If the plants don't make it then we'll do the seeds in spring."

The old garden had raised beds and was situated on quite a hill. The new site was nice and flat. So we started digging holes twice the size of what we expected the root balls to be for the herb, plant, and flower transplants. We built up the soil for purple coneflower and comfrey in the new garden, making a raised bed for easy harvesting of its roots later. Then we started putting down the straw, making paths and placing it all around the areas where the new plants and herbs would soon be. For the Chinese cabbage plants that were already pretty big, I took bales of straw and surrounded an area of 2 square feet inside the space where I had dug holes for the plants.

On an overcast evening, we began to dig up the plants at the old farm. Many of the herbs were cut back and lots were hung to dry. We watered the remaining herbs and plants very well before starting to dig. Keeping as much of the dirt intact, I carefully dug up the plants and put them in buckets, bags, or whatever was large enough and strong enough to hold the important cargo. We dug coneflower, rosemary, clary sage, parsley, garlic chives, horehound, elecampane, lavender, celery, catnip, hyssop, bee balm, and more than I can even recall. Then we transported our green goods to their new home, where holes were dug and ready for them. We watered the holes, and placed the herbs, plants, and flowers in their selected spots. Their roots were covered with dirt and gently but firmly we tamped the soil all around.

Straw was brought up around the plants again, but not close enough to touch the stems. Mulch, mulch, mulch was our motto. Then we watered, watered, watered.

In the morning of the next day, we watered again then shaded the plants with straw, newspaper, screens, or whatever we had handy that would allow them to receive air yet still get protection from the hot summer sun. For the Chinese cabbage, we watered them and lay long wooden sticks across the tops of the straw bales, making a latticelike roof to hold burlap over the plants as a shade cloth. We experimented and found that it was better for some plants to only be watered in early morning. We began using soaker hoses and surrounding the plants with the wonderful compost we discovered at our new homestead along with a bit of very old, dry manure.

We kept up the practice of morning watering and shading and every one of the plants transplanted began to flourish. In the next month, the clary sage got full, big, and bright green. The comfrey looked huge and healthy. The daisies did well. The wormwood produced a beautiful, gray, bushy plant. The Chinese cabbage pulled through and after a week or so of shading and extra water, we removed the sticks and shade cloth.

It was so nice in the fall to be able to harvest catnip for relaxing tea; sage, parsley, and chives for cooking seasonings; lots of crisp cabbage to eat raw or stir-fry; purple coneflower (Echinacea) for making teas and medicinal tinctures; and much, much more. The plants and people here seem to *feel at home. By next spring, having had a good winter's rest, the herbs, flowers, and other plantings will have a head start and should be ready to grow into beautiful, useful plants, making all that very warm labor worth every bit of our efforts. VW*

🦋 1 🦋

Gardening—defined as weeding, trimming, and raking (by the Centers of Disease Control)—burns roughly 450 calories an hour for men and about 350 calories an hour for women. Besides adding to your overall fitness, tilling the soil can help reduce the risk of heart disease, stroke, diabetes, and other chronic ailments. A University of Washington study found that people who walked or gardened for at least 1 hour a week lowered their risk of heart attack by 66 percent compared to those who did not exercise at all.

—Excerpt from Help One Another newsletter,
    Aug/Sept. 2000 issue.

🦋 2 🦋

Here's a convenient and easy garden measure to make and keep on hand. With a permanent marker, mark the handle of your garden hoe with inch marks for spacing seeds and feet marks for spacing between rows.

🦋 3 🦋

Bees are very beneficial to all gardens. To attract them, plant bee balm, lemon balm, pansy, Mexican sunflower, mint varieties, Victoria mealy-cup sage (*Salvia farinacea*), and hyssop where pollination is needed.

🦋 4 🦋

Spread fallen leaves onto a dormant garden plot and till into the soil before planting next spring.

❧ 5 ❧

Here's an easy way to bank leaves for future mulch. Dig a hole in a secluded spot on your property and fill with fallen leaves. Cover the hole to avoid potential injury and let sit a year. When it's time to rake leaves again, remove the composting leaves from the hole and use as mulch. Fill the hole with freshly raked leaves and bank them for next year.

❧ 6 ❧

Watercress mulch is very good for the garden. Watercress can be found growing naturally around springs and creeks. When it spreads and begins to take over the beach or shallow water, pull and spread on a dormant garden plot. Till into the soil in the spring.

7

Mulch between rows and pathways in the garden for compost close at hand.

8

When dry weather is predicted, mulch to hold in moisture to the soil.

9

When a frost is expected, throw hay or straw on plants.

❧ 10 ❧

Autumn is the perfect time to plant trees and perennials. Be sure that the planting is done at least 4 weeks before the typical first frost occurs. This will allow plenty of time for the root system to establish itself before harsh weather arrives.

❧ 11 ❧

Some say that the first frost will be 6 weeks from the time that the goldenrod blooms.

❧ 12 ❧

The ideal time to transplant starter plants is on an overcast or cool day. This will help the plant avoid shock and allow the rain to nourish the plants.

🦎 *13* 🦎

If you'd like to try your hand at carpet gardening, find an old carpet and spread it out in the area that you intend to plant. When it's time to sow your seeds, poke a large enough hole in the carpet to bury the seeds and allow the plants to grow through the hole. The same thing can be achieved with a heavy-duty black plastic. Both virtually eliminate weeding.

🦎 *14* 🦎

Discarded carpet can be cut into runners and spread between rows in the garden to cut down on weeding. Several layers of newspaper covered with bark or soil does the trick as well.

🦋 15 🦋

Selected a new garden site? In late autumn or early winter, spread a heavy-duty black plastic sheet directly on the ground and secure with stones around the perimeter. When it's time to till the soil for your spring garden, the grass and weeds will be dead and ready to turn under.

🦋 16 🦋

Another way to turn a new garden spot while adding fertilizer is to corral pigs or horses in the area for at least 3 months. They'll kill the weeds and grass, loosen the soil, and add fertilizer to it. At last a tiller that runs by itself—a hog tiller.

🐦 *17* 🐦

When transplanting in hot weather, follow these helpful steps. Wait until early evening when the sun is not so hot. Have the holes already dug and ready for the plants. Each hole should be dug twice as big as the root ball of the plant. Water the plant well or soak its roots in a bucket of water for 15 to 30 minutes before planting. Place the plant with as much root and attached dirt as possible in its hole. Fill in dirt around the sides first to hold plant upright. Pack down soil around the plant firmly then water well. Early morning watering is recommended as well. Use cardboard or a screen to cover and protect the plant from the hot sun the first few days after transplanting.

❧ *18* ❧

Sew a band of elastic to the edges of two large shoulder pads covered with denim or canvas and slip around your knees when gardening to protect your clothes from stain and excessive wear.

❧ *19* ❧

Wrap a folded towel into an old plastic tablecloth and tape or sew up the sides to create a kneeling pad in the garden.

❧ *20* ❧

Weeds are easiest to pull from the soil after a good rain.

21

A sturdy dinner fork makes a great weeding tool.

22

Weed your garden thoroughly in the fall to avoid extra work in the spring when weeds will be larger or will have set seed.

23

Encourage your late summer garden to continue producing into autumn. Cover temperature-sensitive plants on cool nights with old sheets or newspapers.

🦋 24 🦋

Slip a ¾-inch plastic foam pipe insulator over your hoe and rake handles. It protects your hands from blisters and is more comfortable to hold. The insulation also eliminates the need for wearing those bulky, hot work gloves in summer.

🦋 25 🦋

Wrist sweatbands can be acquired by removing the tops of old socks. These come in handy in very hot weather when weed-eating, baling hay, mowing, or gardening.

🦋 26 🦋

An easy way to sow seeds is to crease one side of the seed packet and use the V made by the crease to align the seeds to flow out one by one as you tap them out.

🐦 27 🐦

Spacing of transplants can be done quickly with the use of this homemade garden-marking device. Make a lightweight wooden frame the width of the garden bed and a length of 3 to 4 feet. On the bottom of the frame, screw pegs in at required spacing between plants. When the frame is pressed into the soil, the pegs leave marks the appropriate distance for transplants.

🐦 28 🐦

Cleanup begins outdoors easily when a bar of soap is placed in a mesh bag and tied to an outside water faucet. To use, swing the bag up under running water and lather soap with hands. There's no need to remove the soap from the bag to use and it's always there when you need it.

ꙮ 29 ꙮ

Homemade lye soap cleans off green tomato stains when nothing else seems to work.

ꙮ 30 ꙮ

Save those large paint-stirring sticks from the paint store to use as plant, herb, and flower markers in the garden. Label with paint or waterproof markers.

ꙮ 31 ꙮ

Here are two other ways to beat the heat when working outdoors: Wear a wet bandana loosely around your neck or place a wet washcloth on top of your head underneath your straw hat. Rewet as needed. (One Floridian we know mows the lawn in the summer with ice cubes in his pants pockets!)

🐦 *32* 🐦

To avoid heat exhaustion in hot weather, reserve weeding or long hours in the garden for the morning or early evening.

🐦 *33* 🐦

Freeze water in plastic juice or milk jugs. Carry along a frozen jug when you expect to stay outdoors in the heat for an hour or more. As the ice begins to melt, you'll have refreshing ice water on hand.

❧ 34 ❧

Rock salt is an old-fashioned weed killer and quite economical, too. Sprinkle it on cracks in walkways or wherever unwanted weeds grow. Beware! Rock salt makes the ground sterile. Keep it away from your vegetable garden or plush lawn.

❧ 35 ❧

Next time there's a lightning storm in your area, consider it a blessing. Nitrogen is released into the soil, giving a boost to the garden.

❧ 36 ❧

To make a compost bin, hammer four metal stakes into the ground 4 feet apart, forming a square. Stretch and wire chicken wire horizontally around the perimeter. Plant honeysuckle to grow up the sides for an attractive disguise.

❧ 37 ❧

Start a compost pile. Use a plastic barrel or construct a wire bin to keep any animals from spreading the pile out. To the pile add: newspaper, eggshells, feathers, food scraps, dead leaves, old hay, straw, decayed sawdust, wood ashes, hair, and grass clippings, and don't forget the livestock manure. Water and turn weekly. It should be compost in just 2 to 3 months.

38

Leave an old pitchfork standing in the compost pile and turn the contents every time you add a bucket of food scraps.

39

A few things **not** to add to the compost bin: dog or cat droppings, diseased plants, grass clippings from lawns sprayed with chemical pesticides, grease, meat scraps or animal bones, and ashes from the charcoal grill.

40

Nothing beats rainwater for watering your garden site, lawn plantings, or potted plants. Place a large barrel at the foot of your rainwater down spouts on your house or garage to collect rain. Remove as needed to water your plants. To keep mosquito larva from developing in your rainwater barrel, add a few goldfish. The goldfish will consume any mosquito larva and add fertilizer to the water for your plants.

41

Put a handsome old metal headboard on center stage in the flower or vegetable garden. Use as a garden gate after spraying with a rust prohibitor and outdoor paint.

42

A metal footboard or headboard can be transformed into the backrest of a garden bench. Attach to any backless bench after finishing with a coat of rust prohibitor and outdoor paint for an attractive focal point.

❧ 43 ❧

Saving seeds from your garden harvest promotes and preserves the most beautiful colors and delicious, hardy, and pest-resistant varieties. It also stretches your gardening dollar and you can share your favorite or rare seeds with others.

❧ 44 ❧

Not sure whether older seeds will germinate? Here's an easy test and a way to give your peas and beans a jump start. Soak seeds in a wet paper towel and keep moist. Seeds should sprout within a few days and be ready to plant.

🦋 45 🦋

Store seeds in a cedar box to protect against bug infestations.

🦋 46 🦋

Before the first freeze, remove outdoor garden hoses from the spigot and drain out water. Store in the greenhouse or garage through the winter to prevent severe weather damage.

🦋 47 🦋

The herb comfrey is loaded with calcium. To supply this nutrient to your garden soil, work leaves from a comfrey plant into the soil around garden plants or add to the compost bin.

🕀 48 🕀

Encourage earthworms in your garden. Put fruit and
vegetable peels and scraps under hay or straw around
your plants or in the pathway. The worms will do the
tilling of the soil for you.

🕀 49 🕀

Garden resting from late autumn until the spring?
Compost directly in the garden plot. Dig a hole and
bury your kitchen food scraps as they accumulate.
Cover with dead leaves or old hay and water. Each time
you add more food scraps, dig a hole in a new spot to
enrich the soil throughout the garden.

❦ 50 ❧

When using straw or old hay between rows in the garden, wear shoes! Sometimes stickers and thorny stems get baled in the straw. Ouch!

❦ 51 ❧

Is it time to spread lime on your garden or hay field? Spreading wood ashes (potash) give similar results as spreading lime. Store wood ashes out of rain in a nonflammable container until enough is collected to spread on the desired garden site.

🐜 *52* 🐜

To spread a large quantity of wood ash on your fields, visit a local sawmill. Most wood slabs are burned on site. A manure spreader should do the job of spreading the ash on the desired field once you've transported it home.

Flowers, Lawn, Plants, Bushes, Vines, and Trees

Trees take years to grow, just like people do. Often, they are planted in celebration of a birth, marriage, or new home, and grow through the years with us. Some grow up tall, thin, and fast, while others grow thick with long limbs spreading across the soil as they ripen with age as if to reign over it. In the summer heat, there is no place cooler to play outdoors than beneath the shade of a mature tree. From its branches we tie a rope and swing and at its base we play the game of hide-and-seek. Children at play often seek to go up. At elevated heights amidst the long expanding branches of an oak or magnolia tree, a child can climb and scout for the enemy or oncoming ships in the bay. My own childhood tree house was built between the trunks of three narrow, but tall, pines. The tree house was equipped with a unique lookout window that was guaranteed not to break. My resourceful father, who throws practically nothing away, affixed an old metal ironing board— minus the cover, of course—to the window frame and we peered below through the small openings in the metalwork.

Many wonderful hours of creative play and relaxed conversation were spent high up in those towering pine trees. It was my own personal place for hosting doll parties with my neighborhood friends or playing with my cat, Shady Lady.

Speaking of cats and trees—after I was grown, we once took in a stray cat that was a little grouchy and unpredictable in temperament. We loved her just the same and, because she was such a deep, glossy black, named her Velvet. Velvet hated it when other animals arrived on the scene. When our cat Professor Boots had her first and only litter of kittens, that was just more competition than Velvet could stand. So she moved herself into the tree house perched in a large magnolia tree in the front yard of our next-door neighbor, and would not come down. After a couple of days I decided that I best see after her myself. No manner of coaxing would convince her to come down. So, I decided to at least relieve her starvation by placing a bowl of soft cat food into her runaway home. However, I wasn't about to climb the tree with a dress and nice shoes on and carrying a bowl besides, so stretching as tall as I could I tried to get the dish onto the tree house floor while one-eyed Velvet meowed in anticipation. My husband, of course, thought the whole thing ridiculous. "She'll come down when she gets hungry enough," he said. Well, the episode was over with a finale I hadn't expected when just at the moment I thought the dish was at last in place, it came down fast and precisely on top of my head.

All that fishy-smelling, soft cat food dripped into my hair. The thanks you get for trying to mother a runaway cat in a tree! Velvet eventually came down, and I haven't fooled with feeding cats in tree houses since. When I get an invitation to dine à la branch in my son's new tree house, I'll bring along a sack lunch and the felines can fend for themselves. DST

🦋 53 🦋

To have an attractive lawn and garden all year, plant plenty of ornamental grasses. They look nice even in fall and winter.

🦋 54 🦋

To ensure a healthy, disease-free lawn, plant a mixture of lawn grasses instead of just one grass variety.

55

To have a healthy lawn in the spring, fertilize in the fall. This will promote stronger roots and crowd out the weeds before they have a chance to crop up.

56

Want a handsome lawn cover that never requires mowing? Remove all existing grass and plant English ivy, a creeping ground cover. It stays green year-round and spreads fast.

57

A ground cover that's sure to attract and delight wildlife in the winter is white clover. Seed it heavily in a field so it will choke out weeds and reseed itself annually.

❦ 58 ❦

Chinch bugs and grub worms are damaging to your lawn and the health of your soil. To rid your lawn of them, spread diatomaceous earth on the lawn periodically.

❦ 59 ❦

Rake fallen leaves from your lawn as often as needed to keep the grass from being smothered.

❦ 60 ❦

Leaves are easier to rake when slightly wet. Rake after a rain shower or wet the lawn with a sprinkler to keep the leaves from blowing away.

🦋 61 🦋

Gathering autumn leaves is easy when you lay a large sheet of canvas or tarp with tabs or plastic rings attached to the corners on the ground. Rake the leaves directly onto the canvas. Gather it up by the corners to transport to compost or burn pile.

🦋 62 🦋

Like to shred your fallen leaves for mulch, but don't own a shredder? Purchase a mulching lawn mower or mow the lawn with a regular mower with a bag attached. Once the leaves have been shredded, add to the compost heap or use as a winter mulch on perennial flowerbeds.

❧ 63 ❧

Never use grass clippings from chemically treated lawns as mulch.

❧ 64 ❧

When winterizing, don't forget the lawn mower. Brush clean the mower bottom before storing and sharpen or change the blades. Empty the gas tank.

❧ 65 ❧

To prevent a fire or explosion, never drive a hot riding lawn mower into a shed or garage, and close the doors. Wait until the mower cools down before you put it away.

🐦 66 🐦

To keep grass from sticking to the cutting blades of the lawn mower, spray with a nonstick cooking spray just before mowing the lawn.

🐦 67 🐦

Keep grass from creeping in the flowerbed or garden by placing layers of newspaper or cardboard on top of the grass runners. Cover the paper or cardboard with hay, straw, or bark.

🐦 68 🐦

Kill weeds growing up in walkways and patio cracks by pouring boiling water over them.

🦎 69 🦎

To get willow to grow around a creek or stream, cut a branch off a mature willow tree and stick it in a muddy spot. It will root easily and grow another tree.

🦎 70 🦎

To protect a young banana tree for the winter, dig the plant, cut off leaves, and clean dirt around roots. Wrap the bottom of the plant in newspaper and store under the house or in the basement where it is dark and cool. You can also bring a potted banana tree indoors for the winter. It will grow a bit more slowly. Position it in a sunny window. Mist regularly, but don't overwater.

❧ *71* ❧

Society Garlic is an attractive ornamental plant. The green stems can be chopped up and eaten like chives. And, it naturally wards off insects.

❧ *72* ❧

To plant bushes, shrubs, and trees, dig a hole that is as deep as the plant's soil ball and at least three times as wide.

❧ *73* ❧

To help determine whether a hole has been dug deep enough to plant a tree without using a tape measure, lay the handle of a shovel across the hole. The tree's soil ball should be beneath the handle.

74

Just before placing a new shrub or tree in its hole, pour in some water to ensure that moisture reaches the root system.

75

To ensure that your new tree regularly receives plenty of water, once the tree is in place and the soil is filled in, encircle the tree with a ring of additional soil several inches high, about 1 foot from the base. Water will run down from the ring toward the plant, right where it's needed.

❧ 76 ❧

After a new shrub or tree has been planted and watered, mulch several inches deep and as wide as the farthest branch extends to hold in the moisture and keep weeds from competing for the territory.

❧ 77 ❧

If you have access to a sassafras tree, you can make your own filé to add to your next pot of soup or gumbo. See tip #530 for making filé.

❧ 78 ❧

The bark and leaves of the Witch Hazel tree produces a natural astringent for externally treating bruises, hemorrhoids, and minor abrasions. See tip #475 for making Natural Witch Hazel Astringent.

❦ *79* ❦

Don't forget to plant some nut trees on the homestead for food. Pecan trees take 7 years of growth before their first yield.

🦋 *80* 🦋

When deciding where to locate walnut trees, consider planting along a driveway. When the walnuts drop from the trees onto the drive, it makes hulling easy as the car or truck runs over and removes the large outer hull.

🦋 *81* 🦋

Black walnut trees are known to produce a substance called *jug lone*. When washed from the leaves to the soil, it can inhibit the growth of many plants within the area. It is best not to locate black walnut trees near a garden site.

🎋 *82* 🎋

Walnut trees benefit from pruning. Leave a central trunk with two or three branch layers. The first layer on a mature tree should be ideally at a height of 6 to 8 feet from the ground.

🎋 *83* 🎋

Azaleas, holly pieris, and rhododendrons like humus, acidic soil. Do not plant azaleas or rhododendrons near black walnut trees. The substance jug lone is detrimental to them. (See tip #81.)

🎋 *84* 🎋

Plant a fast-growing shade tree on the sunniest side of the house to offer some relief from the hot summer sun.

85

Shade trees around your home help keep the temperature inside cooler. However, they can prevent airflow to the second story. Limbs hanging just in front of your windows and balcony doorways on the second floor might block a nice breeze. Keep these limbs trimmed back to allow air to flow in and feel the difference.

86

Next time you clip off branches from your trees, offer them to your goats. They'll eat all the leaves off, making cleanup easy, leaving little to waste.

87

Never give wild cherry tree clippings to goats, as it is poisonous to them. Also, it is a good idea not to give them pine boughs or cedar trimmings because the sharp needles have been known to cause abortions in goats. Source: *Raising Milk Goats the Modern Way* by Jerry Belanger.

🦋 88 🦋

See the tree—how big it's grown. When it's time to take a family photo, stand the children in front of a tree you've planted or a young favorite. Use the same spot annually. It is fun to see who grows faster from one year to the next—the child or the tree!

🦋 89 🦋

Every childhood should contain fond memories of a tree house. Tree houses can be inexpensively built today from discarded wooden pallets. My childhood version had an old metal ironing board (minus the pad and legs) for a window. The window was safe to look

through with no glass to break. Spray the metal with a rust inhibitor and outdoor paint to prevent rust.

※ *90* ※

About to give birth? Celebrate the event by planting a rosebush or a tree in honor of the new baby. When giving birth at home, place the placenta in the dug hole, and the plant on top. The placenta will nourish your planting like fertilizer and mark the special occasion.

※ *91* ※

Nothing keeps the heat off when outdoors like the shade of a huge tree. If you are blessed with such a shade tree, establish an outdoor living space underneath with lawn chairs and tables and, of course, plenty of cool-colored potted plants. If you have enough room, hang a swing from the tree or place a sandbox in the shade for the children to play comfortably.

🦗 92 🦗

Welcome children to the flower garden. Children love to pick flowers and walk down paths. Make the flower garden interesting and keep the flowers from being trampled on by adding a stepping-stone, brick paver, pebble, or chipped-bark pathway. Keep a watering can filled with water on the trail to encourage a budding junior gardener. And don't forget to incorporate child-sized seating, tools, and wheelbarrow.

🦗 93 🦗

Plant a real flowerbed. Position an old metal or iron bedstead in the yard in a highly visible spot and spray with a coat of rust inhibitor and outdoor paint. Plant the center area with a mattress down of beautiful flowers. Dig four holes several inches deep to bury the legs of the bed to keep it anchored in place—storybook charm sure to please the young and old alike.

❧ 94 ❧

Visually spill flowers out of a bucket for an eye-catching display. This works best on an incline. At the top of the incline place a substantial wood bucket on its side. (Put a rock inside the bucket or to both sides of the bucket to help anchor it in place.) Beneath it, plant flowers directly in the soil. Plant them to resemble water pouring out of the bucket. The flowers at the top should be planted wider and thinning as they cascade further down the slope.

❧ 95 ❧

Set a flowerbed in a diamond-shape pattern rather than in straight rows. It will appear fuller faster.

96

Certain botanicals are poisonous if consumed, such as oleander, elderberry (leaves are poisonous), lily-of-the-valley, hemlock, azalea, foxglove, iris, larkspur, lily, mistletoe, monkshood, morning glory, pennyroyal, poinsettia, tobacco, wisteria, and yew. Consider excluding these plants from the yard, especially where toddlers and younger children would be regularly at play.

97

White crepe myrtle grows faster than the other color varieties.

98

Visually bring forth the dark, shaded areas of your lawn and flowerbeds by planting white or pastel-colored flowers. It'll lighten and brighten up the spot.

99

Grow plenty of nasturtiums around the perimeter of the garden. Besides being beautiful, they help keep bugs away and have edible leaves and blooms.

100

Edible flowers make a lovely garnish in the punch bowl, on cakes, and on the dinner plate. Pick them fresh, wash, and pat dry just before using. Try pansies, rose petals, nasturtiums, and violets.

🦋 *101* 🦋

When going to clip fresh flowers for arranging, carry a tall pail of water with you into the garden to place flowers in as soon as they are cut.

🦋 *102* 🦋

When collecting wildflowers or garden flowers for pressing, carry along an old telephone book to use as a temporary flower press. Place the flowers into the book as soon as they are picked to keep them from wilting and blowing away. Transfer to a permanent flower press once indoors.

🦋 *103* 🦋

Strategically plant fragrant vines, bushes, and flowers outside the windows and doors of your house and welcome the sweet fragrance indoors. Fragrant botanicals to include are Confederate jasmine, honeysuckle, Japanese wisteria, gardenia, lemon verbena, lemon-scented geranium, spicebush, climbing rose, Spanish bluebells, and cowslip.

🜸 *104* 🜸

Add Americana or English country charm to your lawn. Train jasmine, morning glory, wisteria, honeysuckle, roses, ivy, or other favorite climbing vines to grow up these charming props:

Horse-drawn farming implements
Old wood ladder
Wagon wheel
Wood or iron trellis
Wire, rope, or cord draped around a window or door frame
Chimney
Birdhouse on a post
Farm bell on a post

❦ 105 ❦

Deadheading your flower garden should be a weekly routine when flowers are blooming. Deadheading is the removal of dead or dying blooms by pinching or snipping off the faded flower head. The benefits are twofold. The plant will be encouraged to produce new blooms and will stay generally healthier because energy will not be wasted on faded flowers.

❦ 106 ❦

At the close of the blooming season, consider leaving some of the flower blooms on the plants for seed. Flowers such as blanketflower, coreopsis, helianthus, marigolds, primrose, and zinnias will grow seeds on the faded blooms. Cut and collect the seeds from the dried flower heads by crumbling them into an envelope. Save the seeds for next year or start them in the greenhouse.

🦋 *107* 🦋

When watering roses, always water the soil, not the leaves. Never water after sunset to discourage black spot disease from forming.

🦋 *108* 🦋

After clipping off diseased leaves, dip the pruners in bleach or rubbing alcohol before using again. Burn diseased clippings. Never add to compost.

🦋 *109* 🦋

The key to successful roses:

1. Roses need 4 to 6 hours a day of direct sunlight.
2. The soil should be well drained, never muddy.
3. The ideal soil is lightly acidic, between 5.8 and 6.2 pH.

4. Mulch adds nutrients to the soil, keeps down weeds, and holds in moisture.
5. Fertilizer should be first applied in early spring and every 6 weeks from that point on until summer's end.

🐦 *110* 🐦

When planting a new rosebush, prune it more than normal to help the shoots get off to a strong start.

🐦 *111* 🐦

Prune roses in the coolest months that freezing weather does not occur.

🦋 *112* 🦋

Give your roses a boost by placing banana skins in a spray bottle with warm water. Allow the sealed bottle to sit at least 2 weeks or until fermented. Spray the liquid on the rosebushes.

🦋 *113* 🦋

Pine straw is perfect mulch for acid-loving roses, camellias, azaleas, and rhododendrons.

🦋 *114* 🦋

Save eggshells, tea, and coffee grounds to work into the soil around acidic-loving plants such as roses, camellias, azaleas, and rhododendrons.

🦋 *115* 🦋

Transform an unattractive fence or unsightly wall by training blooming climbers such as roses to grow up the fencerow or wall. "Don Juan" is an excellent climbing rose. Add compost to the soil just before planting.

🦋 *116* 🦋

To make liquid fertilizer for plants: In a blender purée 1 part pared vegetable or fruit peelings along with 3 parts water. Pour liquid blend on the soil surrounding your lawn flowers or potted plants. It makes a great boost for indoor container plants, too.

❧ *117* ❧

Next time you take the last pickle out of a jar, pour the remaining vinegar water onto the soil of acidic-loving plants.

❧ *118* ❧

Azaleas grow best in soil that is high in acidity. Water with a solution of 2 T. white vinegar to a quart of water.

❧ *119* ❧

Time to plant sunflower seedlings in the garden or flower bed? Condition the seedlings to the outdoors first by sitting them outside on a day with fair weather conditions. Do so several days in a row and take them back to the greenhouse in the evenings. Once planted in the garden or flowerbed, they should be able to withstand wind and rain.

❧ *120* ❧

Cover the heads of your sunflower plants with a net to keep the birds from feasting on them.

❧ *121* ❧

Sunflower seeds are ready to harvest when the flower petals start to fall off. The heads will start to droop and the backs begin to turn a yellowish brown.

❧ *122* ❧

To collect the seeds from the sunflower plant, cut the head off the stem and place in a paper sack or pillowcase. Hang to dry in a warm spot free from dampness. The rafters in your barn, garage, or attic are a great place for drying sunflower seed heads, herbs, and cut flowers. Remove sunflower seeds from the paper sack once dried and lay between two mesh screens to dry for a few more days before storing. To save some for seed, store in a cedar box.

❧ *123* ❧

A close relative to the sunflower, the Jerusalem artichoke is easy to grow. Besides producing a lovely flower, its underground tubers are harvested for their nutty flavor comparable to potatoes and artichokes and can be eaten raw, prepared like a potato, sautéed and served with fresh herbs, or stir-fried. The tubers, high in carbohydrates, are commercially labeled sun chokes or sunflower chokes in grocery markets. Try growing, digging, and tasting your own. Any tubers left in the ground will sprout the following year. Be careful—Jerusalem artichokes also have a tendency to spread.

❧ 124 ❧

Tired of mowing steep slopes and fighting erosion? Replace grass with a good ground cover and never mow again! For areas receiving lots of direct sun, plant crown vetch, pink Missouri primrose, and red sedum creeper. Ground covers suitable for both sunny and shady spots are evergreen vince (periwinkle), Irish moss, yellow archangel, and lady's mantle.

❧ 125 ❧

Help fight soil erosion on your hillsides. Plant flowering bulbs that grow deep into the soil. Lilies and dahlia are two prime examples, as they require planting at depths of 5 to 6 inches. Planting a slope in a variety of flowering bulbs, including daylilies, bearded iris, dahlia and gladiolus, caladium, and peony will yield color all summer and eliminate the need to mow a difficult region of your lawn.

❧ *126* ❧

When purchasing spring-blooming bulbs, prechill them in the crisper drawer of the refrigerator for 6 to 8 weeks prior to the recommended planting time.

❧ *127* ❧

Daylilies are a hardy perennial that can be divided any time, even in full bloom, as long as a large clump of soil comes attached to the root. Splitting with a garden fork may prove useful. Always cut off blossoms after a division to allow the plant to divert full energy into root growth.

❧ *128* ❧

After those beautiful indoor containers of winter white blooming bulbs have ceased flowering, continue to water them and transplant them outdoors once all chance

of frost has passed. The bulbs should naturalize outdoors nicely. Plant bulb transplants as deep down as its
foliage grows up.

❧ *129* ❧

Planting Depth Chart for Flowering Bulbs

Begonia	1″deep
Paper whites (narcissus)	1″–2″deep
Freesia	2″deep
Bearded iris	2″deep
Anemone	2″deep
Ranunculus	3″deep
Tigridia	3″deep
Canna	3″deep
Dwarf calla lilies	3″–4″deep
Peony	3″–4″deep
Gladiolus	4″deep
Caladium	4″deep
Dahlia	5″deep
Lily	5″–6″deep

🐦 *130* 🐦

Stack your bulb plantings in the same hole to heighten the color and add variety come spring. Place at least an inch of soil between bulbs. For example, plant daffodil bulbs first, add soil, and then plant tulips. Add more soil, then plant smaller bulbs, grape hyacinth, or crocus.

🐦 *131* 🐦

Pansies bloom best in cooler weather. They will grow leggy by the middle of the summer. When this happens, pinch stems back and wait until the weather cools and blooming resumes.

132

Many flowers will self-seed at the end of the blooming season. Allow the flowers to drop seeds before cutting back in autumn. Examples of flowers that will drop seeds are blanketflower, helianthus, marigolds, primroses, zinnias, and coreopsis.

133

Use a small cheesecloth bag or paper sack to catch the seeds as they fall from maturing seed heads and pods.

134

Spacing of annuals, seeds, and transplants should be 8 inches apart.

🦋 *135* 🦋

When spacing perennials, remember that they tend to multiply. Spacing should be about 2 feet between seeds and transplants to allow adequate growth.

🦋 *136* 🦋

Need a ground cover that deer won't disturb? Try pink Missouri primrose, red sedum creeper, periwinkle, beacon silver, Thorndale ivy, variegated vinca, lady's mantle, or variegated pachysandra.

Source: Springhill Nurseries of Tipp City, Ohio.

🦅 *137* 🦅

Deer playing havoc in your flowerbed? Here are some species that deer tend to avoid: black-eyed Susan, phlox, purple liatris, blue-chip campanula, belladonna, delphinium, astilbe, hardy cyclamen, ostrich plume fern, lady fern, caladium, lily-of-the-valley, and daylilies.
Source: Springhill Nurseries of Tipp City, Ohio.

🦅 *138* 🦅

Flowers are beautiful and should be enjoyed everywhere. Flowers with long stems that make perfect cut flowers are aster, black-eyed Susans, calendula, chrysanthemum, coneflower, coreopsis, iris, larkspur, marigolds, oriental poppies, snapdragon, white globe amaranth, sunflowers, spikes, cosmos, roses, and zinnia.

❦ *139* ❦

To test a flower to see if it might make a good cutting candidate, set a simple cut stem in a glass of water. See how much water the flower stem draws overnight. Flowers that drink the most, live the longest cut.

❦ *140* ❦

Purple coneflower (Echinacea) makes many new little plants by fall—sometimes 20 from the base of the mother plant. These can be divided and replanted to start more coneflower plants. Most folks say fall is the best time to divide. However, you may be able to do so in early spring with great success.

🦋 *141* 🦋

A plant that transfers easily from pot to garden soil is the chrysanthemum.

🦋 *142* 🦋

Mums (chrysanthemum) don't like wet feet. They are best planted in containers or in raised beds where drainage is good. Plant mums in clusters of three to five of the same cultivars for the most impact.

🦋 *143* 🦋

For successful naturalizing of mums, buy the ones labeled "hardy mums" rather than florist mums, which can't tolerate harsh winters.

🦋 *144* 🦋

Hardy type mums form a rosette of leaves at the crown when they stop blooming. If this rosette doesn't appear, don't bother setting the plant into the garden.

🦋 *145* 🦋

In extremely cold climates, dig mums up and replant in containers. Winter in an unheated garage with a grow light, keeping the soil barely moist. Return to the outdoors after the last spring frost.

🐦 *146* 🐦

To encourage bushy fall flowering of mums, pinch back buds and blooms during the summer.

Fruits, Vegetables, and Orchard

Kneeling to pick strawberries under the glow of a warm spring sun yields piles of ruby red fruit in your pail and a bright red stain on your white sneakers. Strawberry plants are also at the right height for all the junior pickers you care to bring along for the fun. Fresh strawberry pie with a shiny red glaze and plenty of whipped cream is soon in the making if you can rescue enough berries from hungry little mouths to carry into the kitchen.

Blueberries ripen next and are by far the easiest to harvest—just stand and pick. When the little ones can't yet reach the bush but want to help, we set them up on our shoulders and let them pluck away. Berry picking is set aside as a family affair and one that we all look forward to as each berry is gathered annually. After bags and bags of fresh blueberries have been frozen for daily breakfast toppings on our homemade museli or granola, we almost always have enough left for a cobbler or two hot from the oven.

The wild blackberry bushes here are vast and plentiful along our narrow drive and on top of the hill. In the heat of the summer, the bushes are thick with both fruit and thorns and sure to prick the careless and those that aren't gentle with their touch. Another invisible enemy awaits all who try their hand at blackberry picking. It bites with no warning, but leaves plenty of reminders behind. Whether you call them red bugs or chiggers, the itch from their bite can be as irritating as a case of poison ivy. Home remedies for relief vary, but an old standby is to paint clear fingernail polish over the red spots on your body. This is said to smother the little critters that are taking up residence under your skin. The fun part is watching the hardy menfolk sit around and paint themselves with fingernail polish. Keep some around for just this occasion.

After the itching has been brought under control, blackberry jam is preserved in quantities to last until next year. Green leaves from the bush are dried in a paper sack to keep on hand for making herbal tea as a home remedy for diarrhea.

A sign of the last days of berry picking is when the elderberry ripens. Here in Tennessee it is usually late August through early September. The berries grow wildly on bushes along roadsides, especially in low spots next to ditches. My husband says that we should have a bumper sticker placed on the back of our van in late summer that reads, "Warning, this vehicle brakes for elderberries," because I am known for pulling our car over along country roads and loading up a cooler full of this fruit. Elderberries are free, in abundance, *and higher in vitamin C than oranges or grapefruits, so who can resist? And after you taste my recipe for elderberry syrup, maybe we'll need to send you a bumper sticker too! DST*

147

Save on garden space by planting cucumbers, water-melons, and cantaloupe beneath corn plants.

148

Use space wisely in the garden by planting the three sisters method. Plant your corn. Plant green beans to grow up the corn, and plant pumpkins, cucumbers, and squash to grow on the ground.

❧ *149* ❧

Plant a tall grass with your climbing peas and other like vegetables to act as a natural trellis, thus eliminating the expense and labor of building a support system.

❧ *150* ❧

Another easy way to trellis your climbing peas is to plant them around a round bale of hay.

❧ *151* ❧

Start eggplant in containers and keep them at least 3 feet off the ground. Wait until July to transfer plants to the garden. This should help prevent flea-beetle infestation and yield a healthier plant.

🐚 *152* 🐚

Have a hill that plants like to travel? Try this method to help keep seeds or plants in place when planting on a slope. Fill a portion of a panty hose leg with soil. Tie at both ends. Dig a small narrow trench into the hillside. Place the leg in the trench. Fill in with soil until only the top is exposed. Slit tiny holes in the top area of the leg of soil and plant seeds or seedlings and water. When heavy rains come, your plants should have a leg to stand on!

🐚 *153* 🐚

A large lampshade frame (minus the fabric) makes a good support in the garden for small bushy plants.

❧ *154* ❧

Keep squash and melons growing on the vine instead of drooping on the ground. Wrap old panty hose around the maturing fruit like a sling and secure to stake or trellis to protect from rot and insect infestation.

❧ *155* ❧

Instead of purchasing wooden stakes for vine plant supports, try cutting down and using green branches or bamboo.

❧ *156* ❧

Reduce excess labor and save garden space by growing Irish potatoes and sweet potatoes in old car tires. The

plants grow up instead of all over! Add topsoil and manure to the hole inside an old tire and plant seed potatoes. Add a second tire and additional topsoil as the plant leaves grow tall. Water often. To harvest, remove the tires one at a time.

🐦 *157* 🐦

Easiest potato patch ever. Pick a spot and set seed potatoes out every foot or so, in rows 2 feet apart—right on
top of the ground. No need to break ground or anything! On top of each row of seed potatoes, cover with
hay or straw about 8 inches deep. Between each row,
keep the weeds down by placing some flattened cardboard boxes on the ground. That's it. No cultivating,
no weeding, no watering. The hay keeps the plants
well mulched and moist. As the plants grow upward
through the hay, add more hay on top as needed. At
harvest time, all there is to do is pull the hay aside and
your potatoes (loads of them) will be sitting there on
the ground, pretty as you please. Earthworms too.
Then place the old straw around your tomato plants.
You've got to try a patch of these.

❧ *158* ❧

To grow clean leeks, use straw instead of sand or sandy soil. Set the plants in 4-inch-deep trenches. Then gradually fill the trench with straw instead of soil as the leeks grow. Each leek should have about a 5-inch white stalk and plants will pull up easily.

❧ *159* ❧

Sand around onions allows them to expand. Plant onion sets before all chance of frost has passed for bigger onions.

❧ *160* ❧

When harvesting grapes, don't forget the usefulness of the leaves. Grape leaves are used in pickle-making and as a wrapper for rice and meat when steam cooking.

❧ *161* ❧

Gardening novice looking for an easy-to-grow crop? Try planting kale seeds. Kale is one of the easiest vegetables to grow and thrives in almost any soil type.

❧ *162* ❧

Some vegetables do better (taste better too) after a frost. Brussels sprouts and kale are prime examples.

❧ *163* ❧

Help young seedlings (transplants) off to a good start in the garden. In early spring, place the top of a gallon milk jug with the bottom cut off over each transplant. Discard the cap. This mini housing will protect the

PEARLS OF GARDEN WISDOM

plant from excessive wind, hot sun, or freezing temper-
atures. Teepees made from newspaper can be used in
place of the milk jug if desired.

℈ 164 ℈

Orchards are best located on a northeast slope. Exposure
to the morning sun dries foliage early each day during the
growing season, thus reducing potential disease problems.

℈ 165 ℈

Locating an orchard on an elevated site provides shelter
from spring frost.

🦋 *166* 🦋

If possible, avoid planting fruit and nut trees close to the house and other buildings to keep falling fruit from staining and damaging the roof and clogging rain gutters.

🦋 *167* 🦋

Protect newly planted fruit trees by wrapping aluminum foil around the base of the trunks. This will help keep rabbits, mice, and other small rodents from nibbling on them.

🦋 *168* 🦋

Drape netting over berry bushes and young orchard trees to protect ripening fruit from birds.

❧ *169* ☙

An inexpensive way to supply carrots with the phosphorous and potash nutrients needed is with applications of hardwood ashes and bone meal.

❧ *170* ☙

Carrots harvested in fall yield a superior taste. Plant carrot seeds about 60 days before the average frost and 80 days before the first hard frost.

❧ *171* ☙

The sweeter tasting a carrot, the higher its nutritional content.

❧ *172* ❧

Darker green lettuces contain the most nutrients. Plant romaine over iceberg for better nutrition.

❧ *173* ❧

Strawberries picked on a sunny day will contain a higher level of vitamins.

❧ *174* ❧

To encourage more fruit in the orchard, plant forget-me-nots around trees. The bright flowers attract bees, which then find the fruit blossoms. The flowers seem to be helpful with apricot, apple, cherry, and plum trees.

❧ *175* ☙

Looking for a fast, easy-growing, no-maintenance addition to your orchard? Consider the elderberry. Plant bushes in spring. Harvest berries by breaking off the clusters of dark purple berries in late summer.

❧ *176* ☙

Berry bushes such as blueberry and whortleberries make fine ornamentals off-season with a beautiful display of red autumn leaves.

❧ *177* ☙

One of the best ways to train a young blackberry plant is on a wire support. Sink two stakes slightly behind and to either side of the plant. String three or four wires between the stakes, then attach the canes to the wires with ties.

❧ *178* ❧

Train new canes of berry bushes to one side of a trellis and the older canes to the other side. This makes pruning the older canes easy at the end of each growing season.

❧ *179* ❧

Berries produced far from the plant's center are usually smaller. For larger fruit, prune back cane tips.

❧ *180* ❧

Pinch off strawberry runners for a smaller yield with large fruit. Or let them grow if a heavier yield of smaller fruit is desired.

🦋 *181* 🦋

The Alpine strawberry is a tiny strawberry variety that makes a great cereal, yogurt, or ice-cream topping. It yields intensely sweet yet tiny strawberries, no need to slice these.

🦋 *182* 🦋

When harvesting blackberries and/or raspberries, don't forget to pick and dry some of the leaves. Both are used to make herbal teas as a natural home remedy for diarrhea. Enjoy the berries with a cup of herbal tea. Harvest the leaves only while green before any sign of withering.

🦋 *183* 🦋

It's best not to fertilize raspberries late in the season, as it will promote new growth that will be killed by the first severe frost.

🦋 *184* 🦋

No garden fence? Create a barrier to keep most wildlife and stray pets out of your garden by planting a hedge-row of thorny blackberry bushes along the garden perimeter or property line.

🦋 *185* 🦋

Watermelon seedlings grown indoors and transplanted generally yield one-third more fruit than those sown directly into the garden.

🦋 *186* 🦋

Don't overwater watermelon plants, even in a drought. Watermelons will become sweeter than usual under hot, dry conditions.

🦋 *187* 🦋

Watermelon and cantaloupe can be cut into chunks and frozen for making refreshing smoothies all year long.

🦋 *188* 🦋

Country folk often plunge surplus watermelon into the spring branch or creek to chill. If you do so, turn often, checking for signs of crayfish. They'll chisel holes in your melon and ruin it.

🦋 *189* 🦋

If you want to try to grow one really large pumpkin, cut off all the blossoms from the plant except two.

🦋 *190* 🦋

Sow bean seeds eye-down for best germination.

🦋 *191* 🦋

Grow your own gourmet mix of Mesclun. Mesclun is a fancy mix of lettuces served in fine gourmet restaurants. Blend at least five varieties of lettuce seeds, then plant. Here's a good mix to try:

1 seed packet of curly endive
1 seed packet of red lettuce
1 seed packet of romaine lettuce

1 seed packet of arugula or mâche
2 seed packets of salad bowl or black-seeded Simpson
lettuce
Source: In your garden flyer, Wal-Mart Gardens.

❧ *192* ❧

When harvesting cabbage, cut off the head, leaving stem and the rest of the plant intact. Soon the cabbage plant will grow smaller, but great-tasting, cabbages out of the sides of the stems.

❧ *193* ❧

Cut large bottom leaves off okra plants to prompt more pods and protect your arms from itching when picking mature okra. To remove okra stickers or prickles from the skin, apply duct or scotch tape and pull off quickly. Soothe okra prickles on the skin with an application of aloe.

🐦 *194* 🐦

Beets are sensitive to deficiencies of trace elements. If homegrown beets don't taste sweet or tender, a lack of boron or other trace element may be the cause. Boron can be supplied by sprinkling borax very lightly over the soil. Trace elements or a dried seaweed product can be added to the soil with greens.

🐦 *195* 🐦

Plant cherry tomatoes in your garden as they generally ripen quicker than regular tomatoes. The skins are thicker, too, and therefore not as susceptible to insect damage.

🦋 *196* 🦋

To save tomato seed like rainbow or mini bussell and other open-pollinated seed, try the following: Cut open a tomato. Let the juice and seeds fall on a newspaper. Spread it out a bit so the seeds will have plenty of room to dry well. When very dry, chip the seeds off the newspaper and put in a container and freeze until next year. Or, if you prefer, once the newspaper and seeds are very dry, just fold the newspaper containing the seeds and store with your other seeds until next planting season. Don't forget to label the variety.

🦋 *197* 🦋

Want to give your tomatoes and peppers a real boost? Water plants periodically with ¼ c. Epsom salts dissolved in a watering can full of water.

🐉 *198* 🐉

Soil too hard to shovel and you've got no tiller? Plant one standard tomato plant or two cherry or grape tomato plants directly in a 5-gallon bag of manure. Lay the plastic bag of manure flat on the ground in a semi-shaded location to keep it from drying out. Make a slit in the top of the bag and plant directly into the manure. Water daily to keep moist.

🐉 *199* 🐉

Fully ripened peppers that turn vivid red, yellow, or orange are more nutritious, boasting ten times the Vitamin A and almost twice the Vitamin C of a green pepper.

🦋 *200* 🦋

To raise colored hot or bell peppers, stake or cage the young plants. The branches are somewhat brittle and grow heavy with fruit, needing extra support. The wire cages sold for raising tomatoes work perfectly for peppers.

🦋 *201* 🦋

Dry summer predicted? Peppers do really well in dry conditions, especially when mulched.

🦋 *202* 🦋

Seeds from overripe peppers (colored peppers) are the best for starting pepper seedlings next spring.

❦ 203 ❦

Adding banana peels to the soil helps tomato and green pepper plants to thrive. Banana peels contain potash and phosphorus. Chop peels and place several pieces into the hole before planting the seedlings and you'll have strong trunks and stems on your plants.

❦ 204 ❦

If your garden peppers, eggplants, or tomatoes have blossom-end rot, this may be a sign of a lack of calcium in the soil. See tip #203 or sprinkle the base of the plant with lime and mulch heavily.

❦ 205 ❦

Lettuce and spinach can get by with as little as 2 to 4 hours of sunlight a day.

❦ 206 ❦

A fun crop to raise along a garden fence or trellis is loofah sponges. Plant seeds in spring after all chance of freezing weather has passed. As the loofah matures on the vine, leave it to dry and turn brown. Then pick the loofahs and store in a dry place until needed or peel off the outer layer to expose the loofah sponge inside. Save all the seeds inside for next year's planting. See tip #494 for making a loofah bath scrubber.

❧ 207 ❧

Loofah, sometimes spelled luffa, is also known as the Chinese okra (cee gwa). It can be eaten in its young stage at a length of 6 inches or so. The vines make lots of fruit and grow very well in hot weather. Cut the young fruits into small pieces and stir-fry with chicken and cashews.

❧ 208 ❧

Harvest Jerusalem artichokes in January and February. They taste better at that time. Around March, when they start to grow again, the taste won't be as favorable. Any tubers left in the ground will sprout again the following year.

🦚 *209* 🦚

One way to make children feel helpful and at home in the garden is to encourage them to bring their wagon to help during hauling, weeding, and harvesting times. Many garden centers and farmer's co-ops carry child-size wheelbarrows and gardening tools.

🦚 *210* 🦚

A fun project for your children is to allow them to scratch a short name or design in a young pumpkin, gourd, or squash with a heavy nail. As the pumpkin matures on the vine, the scratch will scar and the name will stretch and remain visible.

🐉 *211* 🐉

Another way to make gardening fun for children is to let them scratch their name or initials into the soil with a stick. Then sow lettuce, spinach, or other quick-sprouting seeds according to package directions along the lines they've drawn.

Herbs

One of the most strikingly beautiful plants in my garden is the purple coneflower, also known as Echinacea. In summer, butterflies flock to it for nectar. In fall and winter, goldfinches and other birds eat the dried seed from its bristlelike seed head. Family and friends always compliment this attractive perennial in my herb garden.

You would think that its aesthetic impact alone would be enough of a reason to plant Echinacea, but this purple beauty has a greater service to man and animal. The Echinacea plant is high in minerals, iron, selenium, zinc, manganese, and silicon. It contains vitamins A, C, and E and other helpful nutrients. Its properties stimulate certain white blood cells. Echinacea is known as the immune system defender. It has anti-inflammatory and antiviral properties. It is good for the lymphatic system, and is useful in treating colds, flu, and other infectious illnesses. It is also helpful in treating snakebites and spider bites. Modern research is finding out even more.

What a plant! Echinacea is so useful and easy to grow in many areas of the United States. It grows from the prairie states northward to Pennsylvania. Flowering time is June through October. Echinacea seems to like somewhat sandy or rocky soil and good drainage. You can plant your small starts of coneflower in early spring in full sun. By next spring the "mother plant" should have as many as twenty "babies," which can be gently separated or pulled and re-planted. (I have done this successfully in early spring but some say to do this in the fall.)

Space your starts about 2 feet apart as they grow into very large plants. You may want to put all the coneflowers in raised beds—it makes it a lot easier to harvest the roots. Pests seldom bother coneflower. It does not require extra watering, unless there is a drought, and even then it seems to make it through. Cutting blooms as they come along will encourage more and longer lasting blooms. Purple coneflower is beautiful in fresh-cut flower arrangements. In fall the plant dies back. In winter, I've put leaves, straw, or hay over plants and they seem to do fine here in middle Tennessee.

When the plant is at least 2 to 3 years old, it is ready to harvest for medicinal use. Save the large blackish seed heads for seed to plant in the spring. Don't forget to save some seed heads for the birds during winter. For your portion, cut stems and leaves and dig the roots. Wash the roots and pat dry. Cut them into small pieces while still fresh, then leave them to dry. After the roots are thoroughly dry, put them in a clean jar with a lid and store in a dark place. The roots and dried herb may last up to a year like this, but as a tincture, the Echinacea can last up to 3 years. Our family likes the glyc-

erin tincture. The beautiful flower that we admired all summer is the same flower that we are grateful for all winter for its healing properties and we use it often to keep colds and flu away through tinctures and teas. Just before spring comes again I go to the coneflower bed, push away leaves, and scratch away a little dirt. There may be a few small green leaves waking up from their sleep. And when they are ready I gently divide the tiny offshoots and replant them. As spring slowly warms the earth I wait and watch for the little plants to grow into tall mature plants with plenty of dark green leaves and the stately purple coneflower. VW

212

Herbs are great to grow because they rarely suffer from disease. In addition, they are hardly affected by pests or insects. The two known pests to herbs are butterfly larvae and grasshoppers.

℁ *213* ℁

Herbs make wonderful teas, are beneficial in home remedies, bath and beauty aids, and are useful in pot-pourri and pressed floral designs. Pick herbs in the morning and before they begin flowering (going to seed) as the taste bitters.

℁ *214* ℁

Herbal bath and beauty aids containing:

Antiseptic qualities are: lavender, thyme, peppermint, and eucalyptus.

Astringent qualities are: sage, yarrow, milfoil, comfrey root, strawberry leaves or root, and nettle.

Calming qualities are: fragrant valerian, marjoram, hops, and passionflower.

Cleansing qualities (especially for oily skin) are: lovage, milfoil, lemon grass, and geranium leaves.

Healing qualities are: comfrey, peppermint, milfoil, chamomile flowers, elderflowers, linden flowers, rosemary, and lovage.

❧ 215 ❧

Lovage is one of the best bath herbs. It cleanses, deodorizes, and heals.

❧ 216 ❧

Herbs for the nursing mom include:

Borage—drink a tea of borage leaves to increase the storage of milk in the breast.

Dill—relieves gas. Also okay to feed mild dill tea to infants. Bruise a teaspoonful of the seeds and steep them in a ½ c. of boiling water, then strain. Cool before administering to infants.

Caraway—Caraway oil or tea will promote the secretion of milk. Add a few drops of the essential oil to any herb drink.

Fennel—encourages milk flow.

Fenugreek—Drink unstrained tea to increase milk flow or breast milk.

Parsley—Bruise the leaves then apply them to hardened or knotty breasts and swollen glands. Or apply a cloth dipped into strong parsley tea to hardened breast glands.

❧ *217* ❧

Turn an old wood ladder into a mini herb garden. Lay it flat on the ground. Add a thin layer of manure between each rung and fill with topsoil. Plant a different herb between each rung.

❧ *218* ❧

When planning the herb garden, it's best to grow mint varieties in a raised bed or wood box alone as they tend to spread and take over an area.

❧ *219* ❧

Most herbs thrive on a minimum of 5 hours of direct sunlight daily. Herbs that thrive well in partial shade are rosemary, mint varieties, parsley, and bay (see tip #220). Lemon balm does well when placed in a partial or shady area.

❧ *220* ❧

Bay (*Laurus nobilis*), an evergreen tree grown for its flavorful leaves, can be raised in containers and brought indoors during cold weather. The leaves can be picked and used fresh or dried year-round in soups, spaghetti sauce, and stews. It prefers full or filtered sun.

❧ *221* ❧

Spruce up your outdoor water faucet by planting watermint, peppermint, or spearmint under a faucet. Mint likes water and will thrive thanks to the drips.

❧ *222* ❧

Raised beds are advised for growing herbs for proper drainage.

❧ *223* ❧

The easiest and surest way to grow herbs is to allow them to grow naturally as they do in the wild. Using a copy of your land survey as a guide, draw a map of your land. As you locate herbs growing naturally, write the names of the herbs on the map in the existing location.

Harvest as needed, but always be sure to leave some behind for future availability.

❧ 224 ❧

Cut, nip, and prune herbs regularly to stimulate continued growth. Cut chive 1 inch from the base of the plant.

❧ 225 ❧

Ideally, the herb garden can be planted in autumn, because it is only weather-sensitive to dry winds. Snowfall creates a blanket of protection for the herbs. In fact, many herbs will continue to grow beneath the snow.

☙ 226 ❧

Don't trim back or harvest herbs just before a frost. Clipping causes new growth, which weakens plants, causing susceptibility to winter damage.

☙ 227 ❧

To protect herbs from winter wind damage, plant them on the south or west side of the house, garage, or other building.

☙ 228 ❧

A strong serving fork, such as a two-prong meat fork, works well when harvesting root herbs. Just loosen the dirt with the fork from plants and stem and work down, scraping the dirt and rocks away, while saving the roots.

❧ 229 ❧

Thyme is difficult to grow in the south. The key to growing it successfully is to plant it in containers or on a slope where it can cascade onto rocks, etc., not directly touching the ground.

❧ 230 ❧

Ginseng is a great medicinal cash crop. It is the most valuable herb the world has ever known. It can be found growing in the wild on shady north slopes or raised from seed in 90% shaded beds.

❧ 231 ❧

A ¼-acre garden of ginseng should yield an annual income exceeding $10,000! A person working full-time in other endeavors should be able to take on this size garden in addition to other employment. A full-time ginseng grower should be able to handle a 3-acre garden with some help during weeding and picking time.

❧ 232 ❧

Parsley serves as an ideal border in a traditional foursquare herb garden. The garden is equally divided into 4 sections in a + or x design. Wood or plantings such as parsley can be used to divide the sections attractively.

❧ 233 ❧

The root of Echinacea can be used as an herbal remedy when the plant is 2 or 3 years old.

🦋 234 🦋

To test an Echinacea root for its potency, some say to dig up a bit of the root, clean it off, and give it a bite. If it makes your tongue and mouth tingle, it's ready to use.

🦋 235 🦋

When growing Echinacea (purple coneflower) for its roots, grow in raised beds. This makes the harvesting much easier.

🦋 236 🦋

Earthworms are attracted to valerian due to its phosphorus content. Plant it in both the herb and vegetable gardens to attract every gardener's friend, the earthworm.

🐉 237 🐉

Only harvest young, green herbal leaves for making teas. Never use herb leaves that are starting to wilt or turn brown.

🐉 238 🐉

Climbing rosemary is easy to get growing up a woodsy trellis. Place a small trellis directly in a wood or clay box with the rosemary.

🐉 239 🐉

Rosemary can be successfully grown in containers. Bring rosemary indoors for winter if weather is expected to be extra cold. The roots must not freeze. In warmer areas, it can be left outdoors if protected with mulch, leaves, etc. With a little effort, rosemary can be trimmed and shaped into a lovely tree topiary.

🦋 240 🦋

When space is limited, the cucumber-flavored herb, borage, is ideal. It is so beautiful with its pink and blue blooms right on the same plant. It attracts both honeybees and hummingbirds. Its young leaves can be used fresh in both green and gelatin salads. The edible blossoms make a showy garnish on cream soups, garden salads, in iced summer beverages, or in stuffed eggs. Borage is also self-seeding.

🦋 241 🦋

Lamb's-quarter is often thought of as a weed. Yet it is packed with nutrition and tastes similar to fresh spinach. To cook, steam, stir-fry, boil, or eat raw in salads. The young tender leaves taste best. When the spinach in your garden has stopped producing, lamb's-quarter will still be growing.

242

The herb comfrey is loaded with calcium, potassium, phosphorus, and vitamins. To supply its nutrients to your garden soil, bury leaves from a comfrey plant around garden plants or add to your compost bin.

243

Comfrey is an easy herb to grow. Plant starts can be acquired from root clippings in spring or autumn. Comfrey can be divided more than once a season due to its rapid growth and tendency to spread. Comfrey can also be used as feed for your livestock.

🦋 244 🦋

Grow Roman chamomile in paths along stepping-stones in the garden. It has a sweet apple smell that is released when walked on.

🦋 245 🦋

Never buy pepper again. Grow your own cayenne pepper. It's prolific and very easy to grow. Dry it and powder it in a coffee grinder. Use instead of black pepper on most foods. (See tip #542 for making Cayenne Pepper Sauce.)

🦋 246 🦋

Most culinary herbs become stronger in flavor once dried. Therefore, use three times the amount of fresh herbs than when seasoning with dried. Rosemary is best used when fresh, however, and is an exception.

🦋 247 🦋

Chamomile has a soothing effect on digestion. An ideal time to enjoy the apple-scented herb is after an evening meal. Those allergic to ragweed may experience an allergic reaction to chamomile as well. (See tip #535 for making a cup of chamomile tea.)

🦋 248 🦋

Both chamomile varieties, Roman and German, are easy to grow. German chamomile, tall and bushy, is an annual, reseeding itself every year. Roman chamomile, a bit sweeter-tasting, is a perennial that comes back from root yearly. It grows close to the ground and spreads out, making a sweet-smelling ground cover.

🦋 *249* 🦋

Chamomile can bring comfort to other herbs suffering from transplant shock or a bout of bad weather. Sprinkle a light dusting of fresh or dried chamomile flowers at the base of the stressed herb plant, then water with warm water.

🦋 *250* 🦋

Tired eyes? Dip cotton pads in cool chamomile tea (see tip #535) and place over your eyes. Recline for 15 minutes. Redip the pads in the tea at midpoint. Chamomile tea can also be used as a once-a-week rinse to help keep your skin smooth, especially when exposed to harsh weather.

❦ *251* ❦

A traditional and attractive way to set up your herb garden is to construct an herb wheel. Using stacked bricks or stones, form a large circle. Using the same stone or brick material, divide the inside of the circle into six evenly spaced pie sections. Plant a different herb in each section. (See photo on page 188.)

❦ *252* ❦

Pinch all flowering buds off your culinary herbs such as sweet basil to extend the harvesting season.

🐉 253 🐉

Dandelion roots, dried slowly in an oven and ground, can be used as a coffee substitute. The medium-size roots lend the best flavor. Combine with chicory for a variation.

🐉 254 🐉

Dandelion flowers and buds can be dried and made into a tea. They can also be dipped in a batter and fried.

🐉 255 🐉

Enjoy dining on a wild garden salad by combining freshpicked dandelion leaves, chickweed, plantain, watercress, wild onion, dock, and clover leaves.

❦ 256 ❦

Clover makes a great ground cover crop. The blossoms can be used to make tea and the leaves can be added to a garden salad. Clover attracts bees that extract its nectar to make tasty clover honey.

❦ 257 ❦

Eating too many clover leaves may cause water retention (bloating).

❦ 258 ❦

Bee balm blooms in spring, but can be coaxed into a second bloom. Check the plants daily after the spring bloom and, at first sign of a yellow leaf, snip the plant back to a height of 3 inches. It'll grow up all summer and bloom anew in the fall.

❧ *259* ❧

Start small when planning your first herb garden, especially if you are new at using herbs. Pick a few common herbs such as peppermint, yarrow, and catnip and learn all you can about them. Specifically research how to grow them, how and when to harvest, and how to use them. Become proficient with a few before venturing on.

❧ *260* ❧

Most herbs are easy to dry. The best time to harvest the leaves is just after the dew has evaporated, but before the sun bakes off the essential oils. Put the small blooms or leaves into a paper sack. Label the contents on the bag and place in a dark cabinet. Shake contents daily for about a week or until dry. Pack dried herbs into an airtight container and store away from direct sunlight. Label the date and contents on each jar.

❧ *261* ☙

To freeze fresh herbs, rinse away any dirt that might be on leaves and pat dry. Remove leaves from the stems and place leaves into a freezer bag or other container for freezing. Once defrosted for use, the flavor will be good even though the color of the leaves may be darker. Add to soups, stews, sauces, and sautés toward the end of cooking.

❧ *262* ☙

Herbs that retain their flavor best when frozen are basil, lovage, sage, thyme, chives, and dill. They can be kept frozen for about one year.

🜲 263 🜲

Freeze various mints, lavender, and lemon balm in ice cube trays with water to serve in iced beverages and punch.

🜲 264 🜲

Chew a sprig of parsley, fennel seeds, or mint leaves to freshen the breath.

🜲 265 🜲

Many herbs are excellent at repelling insects, including: basil, bergamot, chamomiles, citronella, hyssop, pennyroyal, pyrethrum, rue, southernwood, tansy, wormwood, catnip, garlic chives, lavender, mints, parsley, rosemary, sage, and thyme. A combination of any of these herbs can be stuffed into a pet pillow for your dog or cat or made into a tea and spritzed onto your outdoor entertaining area.

🐝 266 🐝

Here is a list of herbs and the qualities they possess when consumed in a tea concoction. To make a cup of herb tea steep 2 teaspoons fresh leaves (or 1 t. dried) in 1 cup hot water. Cover and let sit for approximately 4 minutes.

Basil—soothing to sore gums. Swish mouth with warm basil tea. Repeat several times daily.
Bee balm—relieves coughs and clears nasal congestion.
Blackberry leaves—diarrhea remedy.
Chamomile—nerve tonic, sleep aid.
Catnip—relieves stress and colic.
Clover blossoms—stimulates the liver.
Fennel—combats indigestion, obesity, arthritis.
Fenugreek—nutritious, lowers cholesterol, and relieves sinus congestion when combined with thyme.

Hops—relieves nervousness and stress.

Peppermint—relieves indigestion, chills, fever, and nausea.

Raspberry leaf—diarrhea remedy; relieves nausea and morning sickness when combined with mint.

Thyme—relaxing to the lungs, reduces mucus, and calms coughing. Often paired with fenugreek for sinus congestion relief and to lower cholesterol levels.

Yarrow—remedies measles and chicken pox.

The Potting Shed and the Greenhouse

When I see the old-fashioned flowers such as hollyhocks, Grandpa whiskers, cosmos, and roses, or when I smell certain herbs like sage and dill or freshly grated horseradish, it all takes me back to many memories of my Gran'pa Johnny and his beautiful garden.

As a young girl following Gran'pa around his lush green garden, I knew we would encounter many wonderful things. There were flowers blooming, ducks quacking, bees buzzing, birds singing, and Gran'pa cheerfully whistling while faithfully tending to his plants and flowers. The garden was so full of life. Colorful hollyhocks grew so big, way bigger than me. Giant sunflowers lined the back of the garden like protective soldiers all in a row. It seemed to me that Gran'pa could grow anything. Folks came from all around to admire his prize-winning beautiful roses. He used varied means to enrich, build up, and add to the poor clay soil. He made raised beds and in those beds he would put leaves, coffee grounds, vegetable scraps, and helpful earthworms. Being a fisherman, Gran'pa had a nice large worm box. Vegetable scraps and water would be scattered in the worm box. The worms in turn grew and multiplied; creating a very dark, rich soil, which all went back into the garden. The results were luscious strawberries, dark green leaf lettuce, large cabbages, broccoli, cauliflower, pumpkins, sweet corn, and more.

I'll never forget the excitement when Gran'pa Johnny pulled up the first clump of peanuts, dangling from a fistful of roots, that I'd ever seen. "Let's go find peanuts," he'd say. It was hard for me to believe peanuts were really growing under that ground. Then all of the sudden, Ta-da. They made their appearance. Gran'pa looked down at me with a big grin and said, "You're not much bigger than a peanut yourself." I felt so special! Together and happily we pulled plants and gathered up all the peanuts the garden had to offer. Gran'pa would say, "Come on, Peanut, let's hang up these plants." As we hung peanut plants to dry, Gran'pa told how he would soon roast those nuts and Gran'ma would make nice creamy peanut butter. Yum. I could almost taste it. The old garden shed was now graced with many peanut plants hanging from its rafters. I loved that old shed with all of its roots, herbs, potatoes, gourds, and squash. I can still smell the dill, parsley, and other herbs that hung in that small but useful building.

In the shed Gran'pa would also store the birdhouses he made from gourds or scrap lumber. Out of the smaller scraps left over from the birdhouses, Gran'pa and I would make little boats that we would float in the water of the washtub that sat just outside the door of the shed. The water was for the ducks, but they didn't seem to mind sharing the washtub with us for a little while.

Gran'pa's garden was more than a garden; it was a place of rich warm earth and clear blue sky where the gentle summer breeze blew. It was a place where plants would grow to feed a family and friends, birds, butterflies, and more. This garden shared its bounty, fragrance and beauty with all who came. The garden and her starter shed was also a place full of wonderful memories of a Gran'pa who took time with a small child, answering lots of questions and patiently teaching her how to tend and care for a garden and its friends. Today there are so many fond memories filling my heart and head. I feel so blessed to be able to work in my own garden and greenhouse with my children at my side, passing along the wisdom and love of Gran'pa Johnny. VW

᭟ 267 ᭟

Plants often go on sale just like clothes do—at the end of their growing season. If you have a greenhouse, you can really take advantage of the end-of-season sales at the gardening centers. Plants are often half-price in autumn.

᭟ 268 ᭟

No greenhouse? Turn a portion of your garage into a greenhouse this winter. Construct two or three temporary benches with blocks and boards. Set the temperature-sensitive plants on the boards and hang grow lights directly above. On warmer days, open the garage door for sunlight.

☙ 269 ❧

Not in the market for a large-scale greenhouse, but would like to keep culinary herbs at hand year-round? A window greenhouse may be for you. Ready-to-install greenhouse windows come in a range of sizes and can replace an existing window. A kitchen window is an ideal spot for growing culinary herbs.

☙ 270 ❧

If there's room to stand and walk under your deck or porch, there's room to construct a greenhouse for the winter. Tack a tarp up for the sidewalls or frame in with wood for a permanent greenhouse.

❧ 271 ❧

Paint the floor black in a greenhouse to store up heat in the day and allow it to be released at night when it's needed to protect the plants from chill.

❧ 272 ❧

In the summer, drape a shade cloth across the top of the greenhouse.

❧ 273 ❧

Use an old wood window or doorframe to construct a quick cold frame.

❧ 274 ❧

Help cuttings to root by placing willow branches in water with the plant's roots. Willow contains a natural growth hormone.

❧ 275 ❧

Paper coffee filters work great in the bottom of a pot, keeping the soil from seeping out when watered. Add this supply to your potting bench.

❧ 276 ❧

Inspect your potted plants at summer's end. If roots are growing through the drainage holes in the bottom of the container, transplant to a pot a couple of sizes larger before wintering.

🦋 277 🦋

To avoid transporting any harmful insects into the greenhouse, wash the leaves on all plants before carrying inside.

🦋 278 🦋

Winterize your garden tools in the potting shed or greenhouse. Sharpen pruners, spades, and knives before retiring them for the season. Hang tools above ground level to prevent rust.

🦋 279 🦋

In cold weather, set buckets of water in the greenhouse, to keep the plants from freezing.

❧ *280* ❧

When determining a roof design for your new green-house, consider a steep A-frame roof if it will be located in a region with heavy snowfall. This roof sheds snow efficiently.

❧ *281* ❧

To keep garden hand tools from rusting, fill a small bucket or garden pot with sand. Add ¼ c. motor oil. Stir to combine. Wipe your hand tools clean and insert into sand after using.

🐝 282 🐝

Two more ways to keep garden hand tools from rusting is to place a charcoal briquette or a muslin bag filled with kitty litter in the toolbox to absorb moisture.

🐝 283 🐝

Turn an old outhouse into a toolshed. Place it next to the garden for convenient retrieval of hoes, shovel, spade, fertilizer, etc.

🐝 284 🐝

Rub lard on wooden handles of garden tools periodically to keep them from cracking.

❧ 285 ❧

To increase the sunlight in your greenhouse naturally, cover the ground surface 20 to 30 feet around the outer perimeter with crushed white rock. The multifacets of the white rock will reflect additional light into the greenhouse. This would be very beneficial during low-light seasons and weather conditions.

❧ 286 ❧

Hang a calendar in your potting shed. Staple one seed packet to the corresponding month for each type of flower, fruit, or vegetable that needs to be planted.

❧ 287 ❧

Save the pages from those lovely garden calendars to laminate and use as place mats in outdoor living spaces next spring, or frame and bring the garden look indoors.

❧ 288 ❧

Keep a file box in the potting shed with dividers for each month of the year. File seed packets under the month they should be started.

❧ 289 ❧

Turn your greenhouse into a huge dehydrator. When the greenhouse is empty of plants, use it as a produce dryer. Suspend window screens horizontally from the rafters by chains to create additional space for drying vegetables or herbs. Lay purple hull peas and beans on the tables to dry. Loofahs and numerous herbs and flowers can be tied from a rod and hung to dry in the greenhouse as well.

❧ *290* ❧

Make your own plant markers for your starter plantings that last even when wet. Using an empty plastic milk jug, cut rectangular markers to the size desired. Label the name and date seeds were planted with a black permanent marker.

❧ *291* ❧

Never allow anyone to smoke or bring any tobacco product into the greenhouse or potting shed. Tobacco can carry the mosaic virus. If you are a smoker, wash your hands after handling cigarettes or any tobacco product before working with live plants or seeds.

🪰 292 🪰

Candlelight in the potting shed? Why not? Especially when a mosquito deterrent is needed. Empty terra cotta pots make great outdoor candleholders. Spray the inside of the pot with a reflective spray, white or silver. Keep mosquitoes at bay when you light a citronella votive placed inside the terra cotta candleholders.

🪰 293 🪰

The healthiest greenhouses are usually very clean. It is a good practice to wash your hands and remove your shoes every time you come into the greenhouse. Keep a pair of slip-on shoes in the greenhouse to wear while working indoors.

❧ 294 ❧

The type of flooring you select will greatly determine the cleanliness of your greenhouse. A contoured concrete slab with drainage holes is easy to maintain as it can be hosed down regularly, thus reducing the formation of diseases that breed in damp soil.

❧ 295 ❧

Some gardeners prefer a brick floor on top of sand in the greenhouse, because any excess water and grit will usually seep back into the soil around the bricks, thus eliminating the need to hose down the floor as often. Also, the bricks work as a means of warming the greenhouse at night. During the hours of sunlight, heat is absorbed into the brick. In the evening, the heat is released from the brick into the greenhouse.

❧ 296 ❧

Honeybees, essential to the garden, can be at home in the greenhouse without disturbing the gardener. You can buy them in their hives for the purpose of pollinating your greenhouse produce. It beats pollinating by hand!

❧ 297 ❧

If you don't have a greenhouse, consider adding a solarium or sunroom onto your home. A solarium can be multifunctional. It makes a lovely sunny spot to entertain guests and an ideal place to raise many types of plants while being able to enjoy them all the time. Plants improve the air quality of your home; including them inside is a step toward better health.

⚘ *298* ⚘

Here are some basic steps to follow to conserve energy in the greenhouse:

Keep the greenhouse cool at night. Germinating seeds do need constant heat, but can be easily started in a small propagator.

Plant low-growing shrubs around the foundation of the greenhouse to prevent heat loss. They will serve as a barrier blocking cold winds and snow. (Too late in the season to plant shrubs? Stack a layer of square bales of hay or straw around the greenhouse instead.)

On the windward side of the greenhouse, plant a low-branching evergreen tree to further reduce heat loss.

Line the greenhouse with a double layer of film plastic. This reduces heat loss tremendously.

❧ 299 ❧

All wood used inside a greenhouse should be either resistant to rot, such as cypress, cedar, or redwood, or treated lumber or lumber covered with a wood preservative. Apply the preservative to the wood outdoors and allow it to dry before transporting it into the greenhouse. If you must paint the preservative in the greenhouse, move the plants outdoors, open windows, vents, and doors, and allow to dry before returning plants.

❧ 300 ❧

All metal—screws, nails, and hardware—used inside a greenhouse should be galvanized to protect it from corroding due to the moist environment.

☙ *301* ❧

Stainless steel is ideal for use in the greenhouse. Acquire stainless steel trays, tables, hardware, spoons, and hinges for lasting durability.

☙ *302* ❧

Keep the watering hose and nozzle off the floor of the greenhouse to avoid picking up diseased organisms. When not in use, the hose should be neatly wound around a bracket.

❧ *303* ❧

Educational Projects in the Greenhouse

Welcome children to the greenhouse. Here are a few projects to ignite their interest in growing botanicals:

Olive plant—Remove the pits from several black olives. Scratch each pit with a pocketknife or file to enhance germination. Place the pits in ice cube trays, add water, and freeze. Keep frozen for 3 weeks. Remove and thaw. Plant pits in a pot with a mixture of sand and peat moss.

Sweet potato plant—Stick four toothpicks around the center of a sweet potato. Submerge the bottom half in a glass of water and watch it sprout in just a few days. Change the water every few days.

Egg Head—In an eggshell, you can watch the grass grow. You'll need half an eggshell, cleaned; cotton (from the top of a vitamin or aspirin container); potting soil; grass seeds; water; and crayons or felt-tip markers. After you've halved and cleaned an egg, draw two eyes and a mouth with the markers onto the front of one side of the egg. Draw a different expression on the opposite side, if you wish. Then, place a piece of cotton followed by the potting soil into the eggshell. Add seeds and water. Keep moist and watch the grass grow.

Pest and Disease Control

There's one garden pest that we didn't include in this section of the book but it brought havoc to our garden for years. It's stubborn as a mule, as bold as a chicken when it comes to eating, and it's as destructive to the garden as a deer. Guessed it yet? It's the goat. Goats aren't scared of barbed wire or electric fences. If they can't jump a fence, they'll crawl on their bellies to get under it.

During our first year in the country, we acquired a few goats, and they had a few goats, until we had a herd of goats on our property. Well, we were living on an old homestead that we hoped to buy from our landlords and neighbors. Since we didn't yet own the property, we couldn't see putting money into better fencing. Needless to say, the goats ranged freely and we learned the hard way what a menace they can be to plants, herbs, and trees.

During a visit from my parents, my mom thought that a potted plant in my living room could use a little sunshine. Unbeknownst to me, she placed it outside on the front porch. Not long thereafter I noticed a pot on the porch. Yikes, my plant! The goats had manicured it well. My full-grown green houseplant was trimmed back to a mere nub.

In the front yard of our old homestead stood a tall, gnarled old apple tree that yielded a bushel or so of apples that summer. Excited to make free homemade applesauce, we collected the apples into a bag. Unfortunately the apples weren't brought immediately indoors. Again, the goats smelled an opportunity. They let nothing go to waste either. The main dame of the herd, Molly, helped herself to the entire bag of green apples. She did later pay for her gluttony with a stomachache. Being an informed reader of Countryside *magazine, I came to her rescue by pouring a dose of cooking oil down her mouth, which I do believe saved her life.*

Later that same summer, the children learned how to hunt and harvest wild ginseng growing on the wooded slopes. This provoked within my husband an interest in this highly useful and profitable herb. After researching the subject, he purchased some ginseng starters and planted a little bed just off the front porch of the house under some trees and covered it with a shade cloth, as ginseng needs lots of shade to grow. With the ginseng bed complete and nicely under way, the goats decided they needed to check out our new enterprise. Of course they were smart enough to do so while we were gone for the day. Once it was discovered that the ginseng had been completely trampled under hoof, that was the end of the ginseng venture and we've never tried raising another patch since.

Yes, goats are a pest to the garden, orchard, herb beds, container plantings, and anything else that grows green if they can get a nibble on it. The moral of the story is quite simple—if you've got a goat and a garden, one of them better be fenced in. DST

304

To remove seed ticks quickly from your clothing when working in the lawn or garden, use duct tape. Press the tape down and pull off seed ticks for instant relief of the tiny pests.

305

The best preventative measure to take to encourage a pest-free garden is to keep your soil healthy and the pH levels balanced. Adding lots of compost and mulch helps.

🦋 306 🦋

Insects harmful to your garden plants are beetles, aphids (plant lice), squash bugs, cabbage moths, cabbage loopers, cutworms, wireworms, hornworms, pickleworms, slugs, mole crickets, grasshoppers, corn earworms, ants, squash vine borers, imported cabbageworms, white grubs, stinkbugs, and pepper weevils.

🦋 307 🦋

Plant flowers and other botanicals in the garden that attract garden helpers that feed naturally on garden pests. Garden friends worth attracting are ladybugs, praying mantis, bees, hummingbirds, house wrens, lacewings, spiders, lady beetles, and parasitic wasps.

🦋 308 🦋

When the weather starts to cool, lady beetles invade warmer environments, often the house. To collect them, place fresh apple slices in the infested areas. As the lady-buys congregate by the apple slices, gather them up with a whisk broom and dustpan and return them to the garden.

🦋 309 🦋

Birds consume lots of insects and are a natural and attractive garden resident. Lure bug-eating birds to your garden area by placing a birdbath regularly filled with fresh water. This will also deter them from picking a tomato for the juice. Erect a bird feeder close by as well. Keep it filled with seeds in late autumn through early spring. Thus, the garden will be their existing haven and when summer rolls around they will feed on the insects at hand.

✿ *310* ✿

Keep squirrels from climbing up the pole to the bird feeder by applying a coat of petroleum jelly to the pole.

✿ *311* ✿

Stop squirrels from digging up planted corn with a mixture of 2 T. liquid fish fertilizer to a gallon of water sprayed on the rows.

✿ *312* ✿

Discourage bigger pests to your garden such as the cat or dog by erecting lots of thin sticks in the ground among the seed beds or young plant starts. This leaves little room for larger animals to roam and scratch and helps the plants to get a good, undisturbed start.

❧ *313* ❧

To deter deer from your green beans, hang bars of strongly scented store bought soap in and around the bean plants. Deer do not like the smell and will stay away.

❧ *314* ❧

Dust green beans with lime to repel Japanese beetles.

❧ *315* ❧

Human scent is said to deter deer and other animals from your garden. Ask your local barber to save cut hair for you. Spread it around the perimeter of the garden to ward off animal invasions.

⚱ *316* ⚱

Planning to fence in your garden to keep deer out? It must be at least 6′2″ tall to prevent them from jumping into the garden.

⚱ *317* ⚱

If your dog doesn't do a good job running the deer out of your garden, install a motion detector with 2 light sockets. Put a light in one socket and screw a receptacle into the other. Plug a radio into the receptacle. Keep the volume low enough not to disturb the neighbors. When any motion is detected, the light and radio will come on simultaneously, scaring intruders away.

❧ *318* ❧

Scatter dried blood meal on the ground between rows of vegetables in the garden every week to 10 days to deter deer. This works for rabbit and groundhogs, too. However, the blood meal tends to attract dogs. Sprinkle lime on top of the bloodmeal to repel the dogs.

❧ *319* ❧

Bright orange tape wrapped around stakes surrounding your garden plot has been known to keep moose away.

❧ *320* ❧

Guinea fowl set loose in the garden will eat hornworms and Japanese beetles. Most won't scratch or ruin plants or eat the vegetables as chickens may.

❦ *321* ❦

Dry seaweed added to the soil will improve pest resistance in squash crops and cucumbers.

❦ *322* ❦

What can you plant that insects absolutely will not bother? Onions and garlic.

❦ *323* ❦

Plant some onion and/or garlic as a deterrent around or between all the other plants that insects tend to disturb.

🦋 *324* 🦋

Garlic planted alongside raspberries will stop beetles from destroying the crop.

🦋 *325* 🦋

Society garlic is an attractive ornamental plant that also wards off insects. Plant it close to roses.

🦋 *326* 🦋

Bush beans planted in alternate rows with potatoes protect them against the Colorado potato beetle. The potatoes in return keep bush beans from the Mexican bean beetle.

327

Radishes deter beetles when planted around crops of beans, peas, squash, melons, and cucumbers.

328

Plant basil next to the tomato plants to help keep them from attack of harmful insects and disease. This will enhance the plant's growth.

329

The aromatic herb rosemary is a valuable companion plant in the vegetable garden as it deters bean beetles, cabbage moths, and carrot flies.

❧ *330* ❧

Interplanting catnip and tansy with zucchinis and cucumbers reduces the population of cucumber beetles.

❧ *331* ❧

Plant petunias around beans and potatoes. Petunias
help keep the Colorado potato beetles away.

❧ *332* ❧

Something eating your cabbage leaves? You can catch
these critters early in the morning or in early evenings.
Just take a small stick or your finger and scratch in the
ground around the stem of each plant to locate the
green worm that is enjoying your cabbage. Do this with
each plant a few times or until you have caught all the
hungry critters hiding in the soil.

❧ *333* ❧

Try mixing crushed garlic and water together for an effective insect-control garden spray.

❧ *334* ❧

Grow tansy to discourage ants and aphids from the garden, greenhouse, and home. Plant it around all your buildings. Ants carry aphids. Discouraging ants will help keep aphids away from the garden.

❧ *335* ❧

Ants hate the herb tansy. Add a handful or more of tansy leaves to a quart jar and fill with very hot water. Cap and let steep for at least an hour. Then strain into a spray bottle. Mark the bottle not for human consumption and spray the infused tansy wherever ants are invading.

336

To keep gnats away from your face, wear a wide-brimmed hat. Gnats will not fly under the brim and make a nuisance of themselves.

337

Wormwood repels the flea beetle from eggplant, okra, and potatoes. Put 2 handfuls of the chopped wormwood herb in a bucket and cover with boiling water. Stir it occasionally, until it starts to ferment. Then spray the naturally sticky solution on plants.

🦎 338 🦎

Catnip contains insect repellent oil, and fresh catnip steeped in hot water and sprinkled on plants will send flea beetles scurrying. Cat owners may prefer to try another remedy, of course.

🦎 339 🦎

Shield seedlings from foraging beetles, grasshoppers, etc. by placing a cardboard box over them. Cut the bottom and top flaps off, push the sides into the soil, and cover with window screen.

🦎 340 🦎

Grasshoppers or aphids causing havoc in the garden? Here's a repelling spray you can make. Grind together 2 to 4 hot peppers, 1 mild green pepper, and 1 small onion and add to a quart jar of water. Seal and shake. Let stand for 24 hours and strain.

🏵 *341* 🏵

The leaves on the elderberry bush are poisonous, but valuable for insect control. Add a handful of crushed elderberry leaves to a quart jar and fill with boiling water. Cover and allow to steep. When cool, strain and apply to garden plants with a spray bottle.

🏵 *342* 🏵

Another pest-control spray can easily be made by adding 2 t. liquid detergent to warm water in a spray bottle.

❧ 343 ❧

To deter cabbage moths (worms) from eating the leaves of cabbage, brussels sprouts or kale, add 3 t. cayenne pepper to 1 quart of water. Use in a spray bottle to apply to leaves, stem, and the ground directly surrounding each plant.

❧ 344 ❧

Make a sticky trap for catching insects. Apply molasses thickly to a board and attach the sticky side facing down to a pole in the ground. This will draw the bugs up the pole to the sticky trap.

❧ 345 ❧

Here's an easy sticky wasp trap to make. Pour a little fruit juice into a plastic drinking bottle with a narrow opening. Set just downwind of the garden plot. Wasps will crawl in, but not out as their wings will be sticky and unable to fly.

❧ *346* ☙

Keep yourself unattractive to bees and flying pests. When working outdoors, don't wear perfume, hairspray, perfumed deodorant, or brightly colored clothing.

❧ *347* ☙

Upon first sighting of bugs on lima beans, add 3 T. Epsom salt to a gallon of water and wet the leaves thoroughly once a week until the problem is eradicated. (More economical and safer than poisonous sprays or dusts.) Pour some of the solution into a spray bottle as needed.

❧ *348* ❧

Grow hyssop around and between cabbage plants to keep out invaders such as the white cabbage caterpillar.

❧ *349* ❧

Diatomaceous earth acts as a natural, abrasive barrier to crawling insects. Sprinkle diatomaceous earth beneath growing watermelon, cantaloupe, squash and all fruits and vegetables resting on the ground.

❧ *350* ❧

Keep raccoons and skunks out of the garden by placing a wide stripe of lime around the garden perimeter. Critters will try to lick off the lime and will burn their tongues and mouths.

❦ *351* ❦

Mothballs or moth crystals will keep toads out of flower or vegetable gardens.

❦ *352* ❦

Drop mothballs down tunnels in the soil to run moles out of the garden.

❦ *353* ❦

Flour spread between rows of vegetable plants stops cabbageworms and other harmful worms and slugs. The flour coats the skin and kills them. (Buy it in bulk.)

❧ 354 ❧

Lay rotting boards in the garden and moisten. The rotting wood will attract slugs and squash bugs. Once accumulated on the board, remove and dispose of them. Return wet boards to the garden and repeat process until no longer necessary.

❧ 355 ❧

Problem with earwigs (pincher bugs) in the garden? Roll a thick portion of newspaper into a tight cylinder and rubberband tightly. Set the roll out in the area of infestation. The earwigs will crawl into the cylinder at night. In the morning, get up before the bugs and discard the paper in the trash or burn.

❧ *356* ❧

Keep borers from drilling into the base of fruit trees in the orchard by planting a circle of onions or garlic around the tree trunk.

❧ *357* ❧

A tiny pile that resembles sawdust near the stem of pumpkins and other squash is evidence of the vine borer's presence. Insert a thin, sharp knife directly into the stem wound, probing until the white larvae has been located and pierced.

❧ *358* ❧

To control earworms in corn, mineral oil or castor oil can be dripped by medicine dropper on the part of the corn silk closest to the husk opening just as the silks begin to turn brown. (This hand procedure would only be practical in a small family garden.)

❦ *359* ❦

Castor oil is also said to be a deterrent to moles. Soak cotton balls in castor oil and drop down tunnels in the garden soil.

❦ *360* ❦

Make your own natural ant mound eradicator. Pick and dry pyrethrum flowers (type of chrysanthemum). Add 1 t. dried, ground pyrethrum to 2 gallons of water and add ¼ c. liquid soap. Shake well and pour 1 c. on each mound. Repeat treatment one hour later to thoroughly penetrate and saturate the tunnels.

𝕳 *361* 𝕳

To avoid transferring disease from one plant to another, do not work in the garden when plants are wet from watering, dew, or rain.

𝕳 *362* 𝕳

The best way to stop disease in plants from spreading is to burn the diseased clippings. Where permissible, make a burn barrel by cutting out one end of a 55-gallon drum. Drill several holes in the bottom and lower sides for air circulation. Set up on top of a few concrete blocks to keep the inside dry and the bottom from rusting out.

❧ 363 ❧

Rake and remove any fallen walnut leaves or husks in early spring to discourage husk flies and to prevent the development of fungal diseases.

❧ 364 ❧

Bee and wasp stings can be treated by dabbing a cotton pad with ammonia and blotting it on the sting.

❧ 365 ❧

To treat insect bites or stings, make a paste of activated charcoal and water and apply to the affected region. Cover with plastic wrap to keep it from flaking off. Repeat several times daily if pain persists.

🐝 366 🐝

Get bit by fire ants while working outdoors? Immediately put a dot of household bleach on the bite to prevent itching and blistering.

🐝 367 🐝

Blot a solution of 50% water and 50% household bleach on area infected by poison ivy.

🐝 368 🐝

To treat a case of poison ivy, soak the infected area with this solution. Mix 2 t. lobelia tincture or extract and 1 t. goldenseal in 1 c. boiling water. Allow to sit until warm, but not hot before applying. The solution relieves the swelling and itching associated with poison ivy right away.

❦ *369* ❦

For heat exhaustion, take sips of salted water. (1 t. salt per glass.)

❦ *370* ❦

Cornstarch gives cool dry comfort to the body, preventing heat rash in hot weather. Apply cornstarch with a powder puff on the neck, underarms, and chest before working outdoors in hot weather.

❦ *371* ❦

Treat sunburn with one of these remedies: aloe gel, a paste made of baking soda and water, or soak in a bathtub filled with water and strong tea.

❧ 372 ❧

Lips drying out while working under the hot summer sun? Wipe the natural oils from behind your ears with a fingertip and apply it to your lips.

Theme Gardens

On a perfect spring day, in the rolling green hills of Tennessee, a neighbor and friend from our little community came for a short visit. Ada met me at my clothesline that stood in front of our spring that was running quietly behind our new home. Ada had a sweet and gentle smile that just naturally made me want to smile too.

We shook hands, exchanged hellos, and proclaimed what a beautiful day it was. Then Ada looked down toward the little spring and said in a questioning tone, "Oh, you have tea?" I didn't quite understand. I thought she might have wanted a glass of tea to drink. So I said, "Would you like a drink of tea?"

"Oh, no thank you" was her reply. Then Ada, again looking down, said, "You have some n-i-c-e tea!"

Still very puzzled, I wondered how she knew about all those packages of store-bought tea I had stashed away in the pantry, since she had never seen it.

Then Ada pointed to the lush green leaves growing wild all along the bank of the trickling springwater. Ada and I walked closer to the beautiful, bushy leaves, stepping on a few stems as we went. A strong hearty fragrance blew in the breeze. "Nice tea," Ada once again stated. With the minty scent now filling my head, it suddenly dawned on me that what my friend was calling tea, I call mint. To Ada and many other plain folks, mint is simply called tea. To my way of thinking, it was not tea until it was steeped in hot water for 20 minutes, then poured into delicate little teacups, and sweetened with honey. Laughingly I said, "Oh yes, tea!" The language barrier was broken.

We both pinched off a few mint leaves, rubbed them through our fingers, taking deep breaths as the mint's aroma filled the air and our nostrils. "N-i-c-e t-e-a!" together we voiced, with smiles acknowledging that we finally understood each other.

The way many of us were raised, if we wanted tea, we just grabbed a few bags from a commercial box of tea and poured boiling water over the bags in a pitcher and added sweetener and ice. Or even faster yet, we got out the jar of instant tea. On the other hand, to our plain friends and neighbors, mostly from Amish or Mennonite backgrounds, their tea, for the most part, is grown at home. When these folks want tea they gather the leaves and stems of the mint, wash them gently, then place them in very cold water, bruising and crushing the tea, which releases the wonderful mint flavor. This tea is steeped for an hour or so in a glass jar, usually in a cold creek or springwater. It's then sweetened with honey or sugar and served with Sunday dinner or with sorghum cookies as a refresher during a workday.

Not long after my visit with Ada, I got rid of all my store-bought tea. After all, it was just sitting on my pantry shelves getting old. Now that I'm able to walk out my kitchen door and cut a few sprigs of this marvelous mint when I need it, why buy it at the store?

Mint is multifunctional and may be used for beverage teas, medicinally, as a culinary seasoning, for jelly making, in candy making, in tea gardens, for ground covers, and for garden accents, insect repellents, and room fresheners. Dried mint can be put in small loosely woven bags and tied to a faucet of warm flowing water into your tub for an invigorating herbal bath. Hot mint tea with a bit of honey makes a wonderful and energizing morning drink, a great substitute for coffee. It naturally stimulates the body without the caffeine or any adverse side effects. And on those hot summer days, icy cold mint tea is a real thirst quencher. There are said to be at least 30 different species of mint. From apple mint to chocolate mint to spearmint, a tea to your liking is only a cup away. Plant a tea garden today. Call it mint or call it tea, it's all deliciously useful to me. VW

❧ 373 ❧

Culinary Herb Garden

For convenient clipping of fresh culinary herbs, place a window box just outside a kitchen window, place a row of potted herbs on the windowsill, or install a greenhouse window in the kitchen. Herbs to include in the culinary garden are garlic, rosemary, thyme, basil, bay, salad burnet, caraway, chives, coriander, oregano, dill, parsley, rose geranium, saffron, fresh sorrel, sage, and savory.

❧ 374 ❧

Tea Garden

Many herbs are beneficial as medicinal remedies or as a refreshing cup of tea. To set the mood, plant your herbal tea garden around the perimeter of an arbor with benches or a table and chairs to create a relaxing spot to enjoy a glass of iced tea or a cup of hot tea from the garden. Or, border a small tea patch with cups and saucers. First a cup, then a saucer partly buried in the soil and alternating around the perimeter of the tea patch. Here are a few herbs that lend themselves well to tea for taste or medicinal purposes: angelica, agrimony, bergamot (bee balm), blackberry leaves, catnip, chamomile, fennel, hyssop, lemon balm, lemon verbena, lovage, peppermint, raspberry leaves, red clover, sage, sassafras, spearmint, sweet marjoram, and yarrow. (See tip #266.)

375

Medicinal Herb Garden
A medicinal herb garden could include the following: yarrow, elderberry, mint, lemon balm, red clover, dandelion, catnip, purple coneflower, chickweed, garlic, horehound, fennel, lavender, lobelia, mullein, plantain, red clover, sassafras and chamomile, raspberry, blackberry, thyme, fenugreek, comfrey, and valerian. (See tip #266.)

🦋 *376* 🦋

Beauty and Bath Herb Garden
Herbs are used extensively in both beauty and bath products from shampoos to facial splashes. Herbs ideal for these uses are lavender, thyme, peppermint, eucalyptus, sage, yarrow, strawberry leaves, hops, geranium leaves, lovage, milfoil, and comfrey. See the chapter, "Herbs," for specific characteristics of each herb and the chapter, "Gifts, Crafts, and Beauty Aids" for specific herbal products you can make yourself.

🦋 *377* 🦋

Handicapped Helper Garden
Raised beds, box planters, stepped boxes, and container gardening are ideal for those with small yard space or physical limitations. Remember, plants in containers will require more frequent watering, but should produce less weeds and require less physical exertion or stress on the back or knees.

🦋 *378* 🦋

The Beekeeper's Garden
Bees are beneficial to all gardens. Here's a few herbs to keep those bees at home in your garden: Chamomile, hyssop, thyme, savory, sage, angelica, catnip, dill, fennel, sweet marjoram, lavender, lemon balm, sweet cicely, and lemon thyme.

🦋 *379* 🦋

The Butterfly Garden
Want to draw beautiful butterflies to your lawn or garden? Certain butterflies are attracted to certain plants.

Monarch butterfly: butterfly weed, milkweed, asclepias
Black swallowtail: parsley, dill, fennel, and rue
Gulf fritillary: passionflower
Spicebush swallowtail: spicebush
Eastern tiger swallowtail: tulip tree, sassafras
American painted lady: thistles, daisy types

🦋 *380* 🦋

Other botanicals that attract butterflies are bee balm, Mexican sunflower, Victoria mealycup sage (*Salvia farinacea*), and cypress vine. Other herbs that attract butterflies are yarrow and Echinacea.

🦋 *381* 🦋

Plants that butterflies like require bright sunshine.

🦋 *382* 🦋

Place stones in your butterfly garden. They often alight on stones and sun themselves. Basking in the sun raises their body temperature. This helps keep them active and able to fly.

🦋 383 🦋

Butterflies are attracted to flowers by color. Group flowers that butterflies like together in clusters for easy location.

🦋 384 🦋

Butterflies do not drink from open water. Create small areas of sand, earth, or mud as watering holes where you wish to draw them. Set a wet sponge in a dish with water. A piece of rotting fruit such as a banana or apple will attract butterflies. They are drawn to moisture rather than water.

❧ *385* ❧

Hummingbird Garden
Hummingbirds are a beautiful and interesting addition to your lawn and garden. To ensure their presence from spring to autumn, provide natural botanical nectar by planting a variety of herbs and flowers that attracts them, including: bee balm, borage, columbine, foxglove, fuchsia, lily, Mexican sunflower, petunia, phlox, salvia, sweet william, verbena, Victoria mealy-cup sage (*Salvia farinacea*), and zinnia. Shrubs and vines to plant are azalea, butterfly bush, cypress vine, hibiscus, honeysuckle, weigela, morning glory, trumpet honeysuckle and wisteria.

❧ *386* ❧

Pressed Flower Garden
Do you enjoy the Victorian art of pressing flowers? Plan and plant a pressed flower garden. Flowering trees and bushes that press well are redbud, crape myrtle,

cypress vine, dogwood, and wisteria. Garden and wildflowers that press well are pansy, roses, Johnny-jump-ups, Queen Anne's lace, violets, daisies, Indian blanket, clover, and yarrow. Greenery to press would be ivy, fern, gardenia leaves, rose leaves, bay, and other numerous tree leaves.

🐓 387 🐓

Dried Flower Garden
There are many lovely flowers that can be dried and enjoyed long after the season passes. Here are a few varieties that lend well to a dried bouquet: Victoria mealy-cup sage (*Salvia farinacea*), globe amaranth (*Gomphrena globosa*), baby's breath, roses, stock, hydrangea, strawflowers, German statice, and cockscomb. Hang cut flowers in bunches upside down in a dark place to dry.

388

Fragrant Floral Garden

Beautiful flowers should smell beautifully. They will if you plant these flowers: Chinese wisterias, Dutch hyacinths, lavender, lilacs, Confederate jasmine, honeysuckle, Oriental lilies, irises, pyracanthas, rhododendrons, roses, and of course, most herbs, which are fragrant.

389

Cut Flower Garden

By planting these flowers in your garden you'll have lovely bouquets of cut flowers to enjoy indoors: daffodils, Dutch hyacinths, foxgloves, gladiolus, grape hyacinths, bearded irises, hydrangeas, lilacs, forsythia, Oriental lilies, Oriental poppies, Gloriosa daisies, marigolds, shasta daisies, tulips, zinnias, and roses.

❦ *390* ❦

Biblical Garden
Planting a biblical herb, vegetable, and plant garden is a
fun way to study plants that grew thousands of years
ago. Locate the plant name in the Bible and record that
scripture verse on a marker. Example: Lily / Song of
Solomon 6:2 / Lilium Candidum. Stake the marker by
the plant in your biblical herb garden. Some plants and
herbs to include in your biblical garden are garlic,
leeks, lily, hyssop, aloe, cumin, wormwood, mandrake,
mint, mustard, and rosemary.

❦ *391* ❦

The Mr. McGregor and Peter Rabbit Garden
What child doesn't love the tales of Beatrix Potter? Pass
on your love for gardening by planting a Peter Rabbit
garden. After planting radishes, lettuces, carrots, parsley, and cabbages like Mr. McGregor, hang a doll-sized
blue jacket and hat on a T stick in the garden as in the

story. Position watering cans and statues of rabbits, cats, and the like to welcome all to your storybook garden. And by all means don't forget a bench to position yourself for reading the next adventure of Peter Rabbit.

🎋 *392* 🎋

Water Garden

Waterfront property is affordable for those willing to do a little digging. Here are a few tips for getting a small pond started.

Select the desired location for the new pond. It is best not to locate under a tree, or you will have the ongoing maintenance of deleafing the pond. Also, large tree roots growing beneath a pond may cause the cement foundation to crack at some point in time. Consider locating the pond within view from the house, especially if small children will be at play.

Determine the size and shape. Lay a pliable rope on the ground to get a visual representation of the shape and size pond you've chosen. Move around until you are satisfied. Leave the rope on the ground and begin excavating the perimeter. A depth of 18 to 24 inches is adequate to support plant and fish life. Once the pond is complete and the concrete and sealant has cured, fill with water. This first filling of water will be toxic to all fish and plants for several days. Do not add anything except the water at this point. The water garden will be habitable for fish and plants once you notice algae growth on the sides and the water turns brackish, yet transparent.

393

For a healthy, thriving water garden, plant life should occupy up to 40% of the pond. Ideal plants for the water garden include water lilies, iris, cattail, pickerel-weed, horsetail, water arum, and bulrush.

🦋 *394* 🦋

Mini water gardens can be established within a wood half-barrel. Special liners are available at garden centers for converting barrels into water gardens.

☙ 395 ☙

Raccoons are notorious for swiping koi and other water garden fish out of ponds. If residing in an area with raccoons, build a ledge around the perimeter of the pond so the fish will have a barrier for protection.

☙ 396 ☙

Add inexpensive goldfish to your water garden. Feed them dry dog food and they will grow more quickly and larger than usual.

☙ 397 ☙

Rock Gardens
If your landscape is slightly sloped and rocky, you have the potential for a lovely, natural-looking rock garden. Dig some of the soil away from the largest rocks for

more visual display. When hauling new rocks or boulders in or relocating them, an easy way to add a little height and interest to the location is to position the rock within an old tire. Then cover the tire with gravel and topsoil, whatever is natural to the area, so only a portion of the rock is showing. Ground-covering plants are perfect in the rock garden. A few varieties to consider are ground phlox, creeping thyme, Irish moss, red sedum creeper, crown vetch, and evergreen vinca.

398

Livestock Feed Garden
Don't overlook the benefits of feeding homegrown produce and weeds to your livestock. If you have any dairy goats or pigs, you know that they love to eat their share of greens. To supplement the goats' diet, offer: kale, clover, sunflowers, comfrey, lamb's-quarters, sweet corn husks and stalks, and cracked or whole corn. (Check a goat manual for determining appropriate dietary proportions when making your own animal feed.) Goats love fresh green leaves. Next time you clip branches

from your trees, feed them to your goats. Never give wild cherry tree clippings to a goat, as it is poisonous to them. Milkweed, locoweed, and bracken are also poisonous to goats.

Indoor Gardening and Botanical Decor

One Saturday afternoon over a decade ago, when we were still living in town, I sat on the grass in our tiny front yard pulling weeds from amongst the purple flowering Mexican heather and border grass that encircled the raised flower bed and birdbath. The sound of a delivery truck pulling up to the curb in front of the house caused me to stop my work and look up in time to see a beautiful bouquet of spring flowers being handed over to my smiling next-door neighbor. "Of course," I thought, "tomorrow is Mother's Day." Instantly, I was overcome with sadness and tears flowed. This loving gesture by my neighbor's husband and daughter stung me as a stark reminder of a longing yet to be fulfilled. "Would I ever be a mother?" I wondered.

In just a matter of months, only two, in fact, I became a mother through adoption and that empty spot inside my heart and our home was filled. On Mother's Day that very next year I was the recipient of a lovely nosegay of cut flowers set in lace with draping satin ribbons and a handle to hold in my cream-colored gloves. How perfect. My richly hued purple and burgundy floral dress was echoed by the Victorian charm of the nosegay featuring vibrant fuchsia Oriental lilies trimmed in white. It was as though my dress had been taken to the florist, as the match was exquisite. I carried my dainty nosegay that Sunday morning with all the pride you would imagine from a mother on her first Mother's Day. And the special part of it all was that my son purchased the flowers with his own money and presented it with a warm hug. You see this beautiful freckle-faced boy with brown eyes as warm and aglow as a young fawn was nine that Mother's Day. Of course not nine months, but nine years old. And I was on cloud nine! DST

❦ 399 ❦

When working fresh cut flowers and greenery into a floral arrangement, tape a pointed toothpick onto the stem ends as an inexpensive substitute for professional floral picks.

🦋 400 🦋

Help those beautiful cut garden flowers stay fresh longer. Pick cut flowers in the morning. Remove all leaves that are below the watermark before arranging in a vase. Add 2 T. vinegar and 3 T. sugar to each quart of warm water. Change the water daily and keep flower vases filled.

🦋 401 🦋

Flowers that drink the most water live the longest when cut.

🦋 402 🦋

For a long-lasting bouquet of roses, cut the roses from the vine or bush early in the morning. Remove the thorns and leaves from the lower portion of the cutting. Cut the stem to a height appropriate for the selected vase, then refrigerate in water for a couple of hours before arranging.

🦋 *403* 🦋

A lovely filler to use when arranging fresh cut flowers or dried ones is field cress or peppergrass. It can be found growing wildly in most fields, along roadsides or vacant lots. (Ask before picking when away from home.)

🦋 *404* 🦋

To water potted plants when going out of town for a week or more, fill the bottom of the bathtub or laundry sink with water. Sit potted houseplants in the water for a long drink while you're away.

❧ 405 ☙

Looking for a masculine container to house a cut floral arrangement for a special fellow? Select any of these:

Old metal lunch box,
Wood toolbox with open top and long fixed handle,
Old leather physician's or bowling bag,
Cowboy, hiking, or work boot.

❧ 406 ☙

Three-quart metal olive oil containers make charming flower vases for displaying tall cut flowers in the kitchen. Simply remove the top of the container with a can opener, and fill with water, long stem flowers, and fern.

❧ *407* ❧

Fresh cut flowers in the baby's room look right at home when arranged in a vinyl or plastic diaper bag or in one of junior's first rubber boots. Both containers are waterproof. Place a block of oasis directly inside the container. Add the fresh cut flowers on floral picks and don't forget the water. Or, set a jar or vase of flowers inside.

❧ *408* ❧

Flora at the front entrance of the home welcomes all who enter. Create easy seasonal arrangements by hanging a vintage bicycle basket on the front door with ribbon and bow. For winter, fill the basket with pinecones. Stick stems of sumac, holly, and cedar sprigs in the pinecones to hold into place. (Watch for birds, as they love the sumac berries.) During spring, line the basket with a plastic bag to hold moisture. Fill the bag with a block of oasis and moss. Add water and arrange long stems of tulips, daffodils, and greenery from your evergreen bushes into the oasis. In summer, try a display of crepe myrtle sprigs, as well as any flowers from your flower bed that stand well when cut. Add eucalyptus, wisteria blooms, and grape leaves. In autumn, fill the basket with boxwood sprigs, kumquats secured with wood skewers, and branch clippings of colorful autumn leaves.

409

Try arranging dried flowers or growing potted plants with small root systems in unique containers such as decorative tins, cups and saucers, a soup tureen, milk-glass vases and compotes, baskets, a discarded drawer lined with heavy plastic sheeting, old shoes, coffee mugs, goblets, painted steel cans, and whatever else fits into your decor.

🦋 *410* 🦋

Nosegays—one for each guest to take home as a party favor—can be grouped together to make a lovely centerpiece for the dinner table. To make the nosegay holders, cut 8½ ×11-inch rectangles from lightweight cardboard and again from printed contact paper (shelf liner) or paper doilies. Peel the backing from the contact paper and adhere to a sheet of the cardboard. Roll into cones with a narrow bottom and wide-top opening and tape or glue at the side. Gather small clusters of flowers and tie in bunches. Slip a bunch into each cone and place all the cones into a wide vase. Place on the dinner table. Give each guest a nosegay when the party has ended.

🦋 *411* 🦋

A lovely way to bring fresh botanicals to the dinner table in a romantic and unique setting is to press ferns and a large flower blossom between two clear glass dinner plates. Plates can be made the day ahead for each dinner guest, stacked and chilled. Remove from refrigerator thirty minutes before serving time to allow any frost to clear.

412

Garden party indeed. Serve a tea, reception, or luncheon at a glass table or table topped with a sheet of clear glass adorned on the underside with lots of greenery, such as fern and ivy, and pansies or other flat flowers. And don't forget to encircle the punch bowl with plenty of greenery. Boxwoods, ivy, holly, and evergreen boughs work great, as well as cuttings from magnolia trees and gardenia bushes.

❧ *413* ❧

Pinecones on the dinner table make ideal placeholders. Huge leaves such as the sycamores make lovely place marks when each name is inscribed in gold metallic. Tie a tiny stem of wildflowers to the stem of the leaf with a long satin ribbon. When serving Mexican food,

tie a tag with each guest's name onto the stems of hot peppers. When dining on the porch or patio, bring nature even closer by furnishing each place setting with a mini flowerpot or plant. Rest the place card for each guest on a leaf and stem or glue to a toothpick and insert into the soil of each potted plant.

414

Stack a footed glass cake plate on top of another and pile plump red and green clusters of grapes, pears, persimmons, kumquats, apples, and other luscious orchard fruits as an edible table centerpiece for your guests to enjoy and one that won't go to waste.

415

Add rustic, charming country flair to your landscape and outdoor living spaces by planting flowers and greenery in the recesses of these typically nonfloral items: seeder (farming implement), small wheeled cart, old wheelbarrow, wine casks, boots, wooden wishing well, parlor-style wood-burning heater, galvanized buckets, washtub, crocks, nail barrels, or a hollowed-out tree trunk. Place potted plants on the rungs of a wooden ladder or suspend hanging plants from either end of a singletree (horse-drawn farming equipment) in a pair of boots, hanging baskets, or wood pots.

416

An old four-sided fireplace coal grate with a metal bottom makes a charming holder for potted plants. Use in the fireplace on the porch or outdoors.

417

Don't forget to decorate your fireplace during off-season with potted plants. Lush ferns fill the hearth opening nicely.

❦ *418* ❦

Your fireplace will be dressed for a special garden party when lined with bright gold metallic foil paper taped into place. Set a battery-operated lamp, minus the shade, out of sight in the back of the hearth for a dramatic effect. Fill the space in front of the lamp with assorted seasonal plants at various heights, using pedestals. Wrap the pots in metallic foil too for a festive flair. Turn on the lamp and watch the garden hearth come to light.

❦ *419* ❦

When growing plants in containers indoors, spray them regularly to keep from drying out, and water from the bottom, especially when in a room with a fan, stove, or heater.

❧ 420 ❧

Always water African violets from the base of the plant. Set a round saucer beneath the flowerpot and fill with tepid water.

❧ 421 ❧

Start new African violet plants by burying a freshly picked leaf into the soil.

❧ 422 ❧

Want to keep a Boston fern lovely indoors? Pot two fern plants. Keep one indoors and the other on the porch or in your greenhouse for revitalizing, and rotate them about every week.

❧ 423 ❧

Looking for an indoor plant that needs virtually no attention? Try a potted aloe plant. It thrives under dry conditions well with little water. Aloe's great for treating minor burns. Every household should have an aloe plant on hand. Snap off a stalk several inches from its tip, split it open with fingernail or knife, and rub the aloe gel directly into the burn. The plant is self-healing.

❧ 424 ❧

You don't have to have a green thumb to grow cactus. It requires little watering indoors and compliments southwestern decor handsomely.

🦋 425 🦋

Wood boxes are ideal to use for outdoor container planting. Wood boxes don't heat up as fast as clay pots, thus preventing the plant from drying out too quickly.

🦋 426 🦋

Slabs of cedarwood with the bark still on make great rustic flower boxes. The boxes are especially attractive on a wood porch or deck or used as a window box. Check with your local sawmill for purchasing cedar slabs in quantity.

🦋 427 🦋

When selecting a window box, consider one that will complement the style of the house. Weathered wood or cedar slab window boxes look great on a log home. Stenciled boxes add charm to any cottage.

428

A window box can be used even when there is no outside window ledge. Construct a shelf the width of the window just beneath the windowsill and secure with brackets. Make brackets from strips of treated lumber, or select iron or brass ones if preferred.

429

When affixing window boxes to brick or stone siding, use screws specifically designed for the material. Wood screws will not hold.

❧ *430* ❧

Drill tiny drainage holes in the bottom of your new window box; cover with a layer of gravel or small stones and add a layer of charcoal briquettes before filling with potting soil to deter any odors from standing water.

❧ *431* ❧

Add interest, variety, and height to a window box or other long vertical container. Anchor a U-shaped wire arch into the soil in the center of the box. Train ivy to grow in the box and across the arch. Fill the remainder of the box with colorful flowers of the season.

🦋 432 🦋

An outdoor staircase is the perfect backdrop for mounting numerous window boxes filled with trailing flora. It'll turn any drab staircase into a bower of beauty.

🦋 433 🦋

When purchasing a potted plant, find out what natural climate it derived from and try to re-create that environment as closely as you can. Plants from a rain forest thrive under low light and should be kept moist, so mist often. Desert plants should be kept dry and can usually tolerate more light or sun. Tropical plants are acclimated to high humidity, so water or mist often.

🎋 434 🎋

Don't wait until the first frost is forecasted to bring potted plants indoors. The ideal time to transfer container
plants from outdoors to indoors is when the tempera-
tures of both are close to the same. This will discourage
excessive leaf drop and plant shock from occurring.

🎋 435 🎋

Wash the leaves of all container plants before bringing
indoors to prevent the transfer of damaging insects to
existing household plants.

🎋 436 🎋

In the winter, indoor container plants can dry out too
easily because of the heat source. If space permits, consider shutting the plants and starts in a room with no

heat source. A room with plenty of sunshine in the day would work well. A lamp left on close to the plants should serve as adequate heat during cold weather.

🦋 *437* 🦋

Want herbs all winter to use in cooking or making teas? Bring potted herbs indoors and set on a table or workbench directly beneath a two-tube, fluorescent light. The light should be hung about 1 inch above the plants and left on for 15 hours a day.

🦋 *438* 🦋

When wintering potted plants on the sill of a sunny window, turn the plants every other day to give all sides adequate exposure to sunlight and to ensure a shapely growth.

☙ 439 ❧

For outdoor plants that thrive on sunlight, winter them indoors on shelves in front of any south-facing window to maximize the amount of sunlight they receive.

☙ 440 ❧

Lemon balm, an herb often used in tea, winters well indoors as it thrives nicely without direct sunlight.

☙ 441 ❧

Watering small indoor container plants is mess-free when you use a kitchen baster.

❦ 442 ❧

The stems of potted poinsettia break easily. When this happens, sear the cut over an open flame. Place the severed stem in a vase and arrange with other cut flowers.

❦ 443 ❧

Those beautiful winter white flowering bulbs—tulips, narcissus (also called paper whites), calla lilies, and ranunculus—are easy to force-bloom indoors for winter enjoyment. Keep watering the potted bulbs even after flowering has ceased, in order to keep the plant alive. Then plant outdoors for further enjoyment once all danger of frost has passed.

🦋 444 🦋

Raised beds; box planters; stepped, stacked, or pyramid boxes; and container gardening are ideal for those with small yard space and/or physical limitations.

🦋 445 🦋

Plants in containers do require more frequent watering.

🦋 446 🦋

In winter, container plants require less frequent than normal watering.

❦ 447 ❦

Shade-loving plants usually grow just as well in containers as they do in the ground.

❦ 448 ❦

Houseplant Food—from the pantry (Pantry Plant Food)
Mix and dissolve the following in warm water:

1 t. baking powder
1 t. saltpeter
1 t. Epsom salt
½ t. ammonia
1 gal. warm water

Give to houseplants every couple of months to give them a boost.

🦋 *449* 🦋

Add crushed eggshells to a quart jar of water. Use to water houseplants to add minerals to the soil, especially those needing calcium.

🦋 *450* 🦋

Fresh highly nutritious green sprouts can be raised almost anywhere without soil in just a few days. In a widemouthed half-gallon canning jar, add 3 to 4 T. of sprouting seeds, preferably a variety pack. Fill one-third of the way with water; set up overnight. In the morning, drain off water through a screen lid or improvise. Rinse the seeds with clean water and drain again. Set on an angle out of direct sunlight to allow the seeds to drain. When the seeds show signs of growth, usually white sprouts, place near a window. Continue to rinse sprouts twice daily and set the jar at an angle to allow drainage, so the sprouts won't sour. Sprouts should be mature in 3 to 4 days. Refrigerate once mature.

🐀 *451* 🐀

Own rabbits? If so, make your own high-quality potting soil by raising fishing worms in wooden boxes directly beneath each rabbit cage.

🐀 *452* 🐀

Nature's potting soil can be found in the woods by turning over an old decaying tree stump.

🐀 *453* 🐀

When using animal droppings as fertilizer in container plants, let the droppings sit for at least 12 months before using.

❧ *454* ❧

Houseplants add a lovely natural quality to the home and improve the air quality too. Yet some houseplants are poisonous. Best not to keep these plants within reach of toddlers: dieffenbachia, castor oil plant, mistletoe, and poinsettia. The bulbs of crocus, daffodil, hyacinth, and narcissus are all poisonous if eaten.

❧ *455* ❧

When transferring houseplants from indoors to outdoors, be careful not to place them directly in the full sun. Even those houseplants that were sitting on windowsills may get burned leaves as a result of sudden exposure to full sun. It is best to introduce houseplants to the outdoors by first placing them under a tree in nice weather.

🦋 *456* 🦋

It's best to shed those muddy garden boots at the door when returning indoors. Here's a boot scraper to make and locate along the path to the entrance of the house for everyone's convenience. You'll need a large horseshoe and two wood stakes, some nails, and a hammer. Lay the large horseshoe on top of the wood stakes so that the tips of each overlap by several inches. Hammer nails through the horseshoe and into the stake to secure the two together on each end. Drive the wooden stakes into the ground until buried so only the horseshoe is visible above the soil. Now you'll have the perfect device for scraping the sides and bottoms of shoes and boots.

Gifts, Crafts, and Beauty Aids

The corn plant is truly a versatile vegetable and can supply much more than nutritious food. Corn husks can adorn wreaths, be fashioned into dolls, and be braided into mats for table and chair seats, coasters, and hot pads. The silk is dried and used as a home remedy for bed-wetting. Corn provides an excellent avenue to resourcefulness. Native Americans use dried, braided husks to construct clotheslines, baby hammocks, summer moccasins, mats, baskets, and bandages.

When the corn is standing ready to be picked in the field, everything else is put on hold. The corn can't wait. During our second summer here in Tennessee, our good friends raised a bumper crop of sweet corn. We bartered for some of the bounty, which left my daughter Tiffany and me with several huge sacks of corn to shuck and process. We sat under the shade of the front porch to shuck the corn and remove the silks. When we discovered a plump worm, we threw it in the yard to the chickens that were waiting close at hand for their share of this treasure chest of gold. They were our source of entertainment while we worked. We cut off the tips of each cob and threw them to the chickens too and watched them fight over the corn. The first one to the corn would pick it up and run. Then another hen with an appetite equally as enormous quickly intercepted the first.

Creamed corn is a favorite of mine, so out came the corn cutters with a sharp blade set to the right height. We creamed the corn kernels off the fresh cobs until our arms could cream no more. Some of the husks were set out to dry between two window screens. Later the children and I made a simple version of cornhusk dolls and glued some of the corn silk to the heads of each doll for hair. Two dozen corncobs were saved too. The cobs were quartered and boiled in water outside in an open kettle for 2 hours. Then we removed the cobs, strained the liquid, and put it on to boil again until it was reduced by half. We took turns stirring the huge kettle. Next, we added a half-cup of honey for every cup of liquid that was left in the pot and put it on to boil a little longer until it was as thick as we liked. The last step was to stir in a pinch of cream of tartar before pouring the hot syrup into quart canning jars. The jars of syrup were sealed and stored on our pantry shelves to enjoy later on our pancakes.

Summertime is a busy time when you have a good-sized vegetable garden. And after all this it was plain to see how the tradition of no school in summer was started. Helping hands in the garden daily and at harvest are a necessity for those that try to let nothing go to waste, striving to bring the quality of resourcefulness to the forefront. DST

🦖 *457* 🦖

When growing corn, save the husks for fire-starters and for making tamales, dolls, wreaths, braided coasters, table and chair mats, and brooms.

🦖 *458* 🦖

Dry okra between two window screens. Once dry they can be given (while supervised) to an older baby or toddler as nature's baby rattle. Dried okra can be added to any natural ornamental wreath or arrangement.

🦖 *459* 🦖

Corncob Gift Topper
Save mini corncobs from your garden and make these cute present toppers or wreath embellishments. Let the cobs air-dry well, then break in half. Red cobs are the

most attractive. Tie a raffia bow around the center of the cob. Glue or fasten a dry strawflower or sunflower on each half of the cob.

460

Indian Corn Necklaces
These make a great costume item to wear on Thanksgiving. Soak Indian corn overnight to soften. Using a large needle, string the corn kernels on dental floss or household string to the desired length. Dry before wearing.

461

Name two things cats love? Catnip and mice. Treat your favorite feline to a catnip mouse. Cut an old sock at the heel. Stuff the foot portion with dried catnip. Sew closed and stitch on eyes, whiskers, and a tail. Cut out two triangles from felt for the ears and sew into place.

❦ 462 ❦

Sage Hair Rinse to Darken Hair
Make an infusion of ⅓ c. sage leaves in 1 qt. of water. Steep for 2 hours and strain. Pour over hair and leave on for half an hour, then rinse out. Due to its astringent properties, sage is also used in facial steams and masks.

❦ 463 ❦

Lavender Hair Rinse
Poke clippings of fresh lavender into attractive bottles. Pour in pure white vinegar to cover and cork. Dip the top of the bottle into a double boiler filled with melted beeswax, being sure to cover the cork. Tie a raffia bow around the neck of the bottle and decorate with dried lavender, if desired. Allow the contents to age one month before using.

❧ *464* ❧

Herbal-Scented Hot Pads and Coasters
Cut a kitchen towel in half. Place right sides together,
align corners, and sew together, leaving a few inches
open. Fill with dried herbs of your choice, such as
rosemary, lavender, lemon balm, mint, cinnamon stick
pieces, orange peels, whole cloves, etc. Stitch opening
closed. When a hot casserole or pie is placed on the hot
pad, the wonderful fragrance of your dried herbs will be
released into the room. Make coffee mug coasters by cutting a large dinner napkin or kitchen towel into quarters.
Sew two pieces with right sides together, leaving a small
opening. Fill with spices and sew up. Use when serving
hot coffee, cocoa, hot-spiced teas, or cider.

🐦 *465* 🐦

Herbal Sachets

These are perfect for lingerie drawers or a gift for the bride. You'll need thin muslin, 2 identical crocheted doilies, and some thin satin ribbon to match.

Cut two pieces of muslin the same size and shape as the doilies you've selected. Stitch together on all sides, leaving an opening. Fill the muslin bag with fragrant dried herbs such as rosemary, lavender, rose petals, lemon balm, lemon grass, whole cloves, mint, etc., and stitch opening closed. Lay one doily on the table, right side facing down and place the muslin bag of herbs centered on top. Lay the other doily on top, right side facing up. Affix a small safety pin to the edge of the satin ribbon and use as a needle to weave the ribbon in and out of the doily until the entire three layers has been sandwiched together. Leave a little extra ribbon where you started and finished to tie off into a bow to complete.

❧ *466* ❧

Dainty Potpourri and Floral Bouquet
For the bride's trousseau, use all white materials. For a
Victorian presentation, use a cream doily and lavender
ribbon and netting with a pansy or rosebud bouquet.

Materials needed:
thin satin ribbon
one round crocheted doily
potpourri or scented rose petals and lavender combined in equal amounts
small silk or dried flower bouquet
fine mesh netting

Step 1. Fold the netting to double or triple the thick-
ness. (The thicker the layers of netting used, the
deeper the netting color will appear.) Lay the doily
on top of the netting and cut the netting to the di-
mensions of the doily. Set aside.

Step 2. Weave a narrow strand of ribbon in and out of
the outer edges of the doily. Affixing a small safety
pin to the tip of the ribbon can easily do this. Cut the
ribbon and tie, hand tack, or glue the ends together
underneath.

Step 3. Place the potpourri or lavender and rose petals in the center of the netting. Gather netting up and tie together with a ribbon or rubber band. Place the gathered netting bag or herbs in the center of the doily. Draw up together like a bag and tie tightly together with narrow ribbon.

Step 4. Place a small bouquet of silk or dried flowers down through the center of the netting. Violets or rosebuds work nicely. Lovely and fragrant. Place in the bath, lingerie drawer, hope chest, or give as a great gift.

🦋 467 🦋

Pressed Floral Coasters
Make lovely coasters for the table with clear contact paper, round paper doilies, white glue, toothpick and small greenery and pansies, violets, or Johnny-jump-ups. For each coaster, cut two pieces of clear contact paper the size of the round doily. Using a toothpick, apply a small amount of glue to the back of the greenery and position on the doily. Determine how you want the

flowers to be arranged on the doily and, using a toothpick, apply a small bead of glue to the underside of the flower. Press into place on top of the greenery. Allow drying for 15 to 20 minutes then carefully affix the clear contact paper to both sides of the doily.

Variation: Colorful autumn leaves can also be preserved between layers of clear contact paper and cut to desired shape and size.

🦎 *468* 🦎

Framed Botanical Prints

Pressed botanicals are lovely and a natural way to bring a fresh spring look indoors. In early spring when the trees are full of fresh young green leaves, pick several leaves from a wide variety of trees. Press the green leaves in a large dictionary for a week or until dry and flat. Acquire enough wood picture frames to display each tree species you have. Apply a layer of white craft glue to the underside of the leaves and mount on acid-free drawing paper. In calligraphy, write the name of the tree species beneath the mounted green leaves on each sheet. Frame behind glass and hang in a grid arrangement on a wall in a garden theme room or on the wall next to a staircase or landing.

❧ 469 ❧

Herbal Bath Bag

Many herbs are refreshing and good for the skin. Cut one round piece of muslin for each herbal bath bag. In the center lay a mix of flaked oatmeal, dried lavender, lovage, comfrey, rosemary, lemon grass, and chamomile, or your pick. Gather the muslin up and wrap a rubber band tightly around the top. Cover with a long ribbon and tie a loop around the bathtub faucet. The herbal bag should be placed so that it is directly in the flow of the warm running water when the bath is drawn. After the bath has been filled, rub the herbal bag directly on the skin for added benefits. See the herbal section for the beauty benefits of herbs.

❧ *470* ❧

Herbal Bath Powder and Deodorant

½ t. cloves
1 t. mint
2 T. lavender flowers
1 t. myrrh
½ c. baking soda
½ c. cornstarch

Combine the first four ingredients and grind to a powder using a mortar and pestle or a coffee grinder, then stir in the baking soda and cornstarch.

❧ *471* ❧

Herbal Baby Powder

2 c. calendula petals, dried
½ c. comfrey leaves
½ c. baking soda
4 c. cornstarch

Powder the comfrey leaves and calendula petals in a blender or grinder and combine with the baking soda and cornstarch. Allow it to cure a week before using.

🪶 472 🪶

Headache Pillow
Lavender is said to relieve tension headaches.

Combine 2 oz. each: lavender, marjoram, wood betony, rose petals, and ½ oz. cloves. Fill a thin lovely pillow with the herb combination to inhale the fragrance when relaxing.

🪶 473 🪶

Rice to the Relief Pillow
Select a long sturdy sock or sew two fingertip towels together and fill ¾ full of rice and lavender flowers to a ratio of 75% rice and 25% lavender. Heat in the microwave until warm, but not hot! Soothing to an

aching neck or joints. The warmed rice holds in the heat.

Variation: Wheat berries can be used instead of rice.

❧ 474 ❧

Yarrow Astringent
Facial treatment for oily or troubled skin.

Make an infusion of ⅓ c. yarrow in 1 qt. hot water. Cover and steep for 2 hours. Strain and apply with a cotton pad, then rinse face. Use twice daily. Good for blackheads. (Yarrow or its infusion can be added to facial masks, steams, and hair preparations.)

❧ 475 ❧

Natural Witch Hazel Astringent
For external use only.

Collect fresh leaves from a Witch Hazel tree and dry. Once dry, pulverize into a powder. Add 1 t. powdered

Witch Hazel leaves into 1 c. water and bring to a boil for 10 minutes. Strain, cool, and bottle. Rub into aching joints; apply to bruises and minor abrasions as needed.

❧ *476* ☙

Herbal Head Lice Remedy
Also effective on body lice, skin parasites, or as a ringworm lotion.

Crumble 3 T. of the herb rue into 1 pint of white vinegar. Cap and let sit for 2 weeks. Apply as needed.

Warning: Some people are sensitive to rue.

❧ *477* ☙

Bee Balm Facial Splash
Bee balm contains tannin, which helps control oily skin. To make a home astringent, combine ¼ c. bruised fresh bee balm leaves with 1 c. boiling water. Cover and steep for about 10 minutes. Strain and stir in the juice

from 1 lemon. Keep refrigerated for up to 1 week. Shake before using. As a facial, splash on 3 times a day, especially in the summer, after cleansing.

ꘖ *478* ꘖ

Lavender-Rosemary Skin Oil
Soothing skin oil

2 c. fresh lavender flowers
7 2″ sprigs rosemary
1 2″ piece dried orange peel
1¼ c. light olive oil or grape seed oil

Pound the two herbs lightly in a mortar to release the aromas. If you don't have a mortar and pestle, spread herbs on a sheet of waxed paper, cover with another sheet of waxed paper, and roll a pastry rolling pin back and forth across the top. Pack the herbs into a pint jar along with orange peel and pour in the olive oil. Cover the jar and shake well. Leave the jar in a sunny window for 2 weeks, shaking daily. Then strain and it's ready to use. Store tightly covered and refrigerate. Keeps up to 1 year.

479

Garden Fresh Soap Balls
Yield: approx. one dozen tiny soap balls

Grate white bath soap, homemade or commercial, into a bowl and measure out 1½ c. soap flakes. Add enough very warm soft water to moisten when stirred. (Approx. ¼ to ½ c.) Next, add several tablespoons of fresh rosemary leaves and lavender leaves and flowers. If lavender flowers aren't in bloom, or if you prefer, add 2 fresh pansy flowers, torn into pieces and/or the petals from 2 fresh rosebuds. Distribute flowers and herb leaves throughout with your fingers. Take about a tablespoon of moist soap batter and roll in the palm of your hand, as you would shape meatballs. Lay on a plastic sheet or waxed paper to dry. Allow drying for about 2 weeks. Roll in your palm every few days while drying to keep them round.

❧ *480* ❧

Gardener's Soap

Make your own soothing comfrey soap for the gardener's hands.

Grate up a few bars of ivory or some homemade soap. Stir in 2 T. baby oats (cereal) and set aside. Make a comfrey tea by picking fresh comfrey leaves and chop fine. Put 1 c. chopped leaves in a warm jar and cover with boiling water. Screw on lid and let this steep at least 20 minutes. Add a little of this comfrey tea to the grated soap a little at a time until you can work up a bar of soap. Or place in a soap mold if you prefer. Comfrey is very healing to a gardener's hands. Allow drying completely before using.

Variation: Calendula or plantain, or a combination of all three herbs, could comprise the 1 c. of herb leaves and would produce a great gardener's soap, as all are of great benefit to the hands.

❧ *481* ❧

Gourmet Mint Vinegar
An easy-to-make gourmet mint vinegar. Simply wash one handful of fresh mint leaves, shake well, and bruise with mortar and pestle. Pack leaves in a quart jar and add 1 qt. of distilled apple cider vinegar. Cover the container tightly and let the mixture stand at least 2 weeks. Strain, rebottle, and label contents. Excellent with roasted lamb or in fruit salad dressings.

❧ *482* ❧

Garden Seed Packets Wallpaper Border
Lay seed packages in a horizontal row on a color photo copier. Print paper of your choice. Make numerous copies. Trim and use as a wallpaper border where desired.

🜨 *483* 🜨

Orchard Hook—Tree Pruning Hook
Here's a helpful long arm in the orchard. Cut a long branch and remove all existing branches extending from it except one, close to one end. Cut this branch down to six inches long to use like a hook for pulling down hard-to-reach bush and tree branches in the orchard when harvesting fruit or pruning. Give as a gift to a gardening friend. Sand lightly and rub with tung oil to preserve.

🜨 *484* 🜨

Pizza for the Birds: a Bird Feeder Project
Make a pizza for your birds. Remember birds consume a lot of insects, and thus are garden friends. To make slices of bird pizza, cut a pizza round (cardboard) in half. Punch a small hole in the top of each shape and run string or twine through; make a loop and tie a knot. Spread peanut butter across the entire surface of

each cardboard shape. Next, sprinkle on sunflower and/or pumpkin seeds. Push them down so they'll stick to the peanut butter. Add some red apple peels for color to help give it that pepperoni and tomato pizza look. Add popcorn and peanuts, too. Hang on a bush, fence, or nearby tree, sit back, and watch the birds enjoy.

❦ 485 ❦

Tea Garden Hats
Adorn a straw hat with flowers from your flower garden and hang on your front door to greet your guests. Or better yet, have a tea party in your garden. Invite guests and furnish each one with a straw hat. Using fresh or dry flowers from your garden, have each guest decorate her hat using a glue gun, floral wire, or other craft adhesive. Flowers to offer for this outdoor garden project are tansy, globe amaranth, baby's breath, snowball, hydrangeas, yarrow, roses, calendula, ivy, fern, etc. Or, if you prefer, make up the hats ahead of time and hang on the garden gate, fence, potting shed, or in the gazebo for a garden party. When it's time for guests to leave, offer a hat to each to take home.

❦ 486 ❧

Garden Gloves
Decorate white- or pastel-colored garden gloves with fabric paint. Use garden theme stencils such as lady-bugs, butterflies, birdhouses, etc., to present to the gardener on your gift list.

❦ 487 ❧

The Gardener's Wreath
Affix packages of flower or vegetable seeds to a corn-husk or grapevine wreath. Add a gardening tool, attractively painted or tied with a ribbon. Take a pair of pretty garden gloves, stuff one glove slightly into the other at the openings, and tie with a raffia bow. Attach to the wreath and the gloves will serve as a decorative bow. Wire several dried or artificial flowers onto the wreath, if desired. A lovely wreath to any gardener's delight. The seeds, tools, and gloves can all be removed from the wreath and used.

🦋 *488* 🦋

Outdoor Bird Feeder Wreath
Consider putting together a wreath that won't go to waste. The birds will enjoy the wreath that you've arranged with dried seed heads such as sumac, millet, sorghum, globe amaranth, purple coneflower, yarrow, and strawflowers. Use a grapevine wreath for a base and attach the dried materials to the wreath with floral wire. The fuller the arrangement the more beautiful. Hang on the front door or on a gate or wall where you can sit and enjoy watching the birds feed.

🦋 *489* 🦋

Eggs From the Garden?!
Grow egg gourds for lots of fun and use in decorative projects. Place egg gourds in a bird nest for an attractive display or put in the laying boxes to encourage young hens to lay eggs—it works.

490

Gourd Wind Chime
You'll need:

1 tree branch
jute
8 to 9 dried gourds
hammer
screwdriver
8 to 9 wooden beads
drill
⅛"drill bit
glue
saw

Drill a series of holes around the bottom of five dried gourds. Knock out the bottom on each with a screwdriver and hammer and clean out the gourd. Drill a ⅛" hole in the top. Insert jute through the top of each gourd. Hold jute in place with a large wooden bead knotted in place on the inside. Hang two or three gourds to a strand of jute. Repeat with a second and third strand of jute. Drill a ⅛" hole through the middle of a tree branch. Drill two other holes about 4 to 5 inches from the center. Insert jute ropes and position so gourds are staggered. Secure with knots and drops of glue. Saw any excess ends off the branch to balance.

✼ 491 ✼

Growing Children's Garden House
Grow a garden house with your children. Trace a square on the ground large enough to house your children comfortably and plant corn or sunflower seeds around the perimeter to form the walls. Be sure and leave at least a 2- or 3-foot unplanted opening for the doorway. Plant Roman chamomile for a sweet-smelling carpet floor. To form the roof, string wire from the corn plants up and across to the other side, east to west and north to south. Then plant cypress vine or loofah in with the corn to grow up and on the wire for a roof shade.

🗦 *492* 🗧

Salad Garden in a Box

Give a taste of the garden to family and friends that appreciate fresh vegetables but don't have a garden. It makes a great gift for the homebound.

Construct a rough-hewn wood box or purchase one. Decorate one long side of the box with wood burnings or stencil the words: Garden in a Box, Salad, or Mom's Garden, etc. Or paint the words of your choosing on the back of a ruler and nail it to the box. Drill tiny holes for drainage in the bottom. If the box will be used indoors, line with plastic. Fill three-quarters full of potting soil. Plant starts of lettuce, radish, cherry tomatoes, and marigolds. And you'll have a salad growing in a box.

493

Daisy Chain
A lovely necklace for the girls.

Include plenty of daisies in your flower garden and gather the children together to make a daisy chain. Make slits in the stem of a freshly picked daisy. Insert the stem of another daisy. Split that stem, inserting yet another, and continue until the chain is of desired length. These make beautiful chains to encircle a punch bowl, a table runner embellishment, or simply to make necklaces for the girls at play.

494

Loofah Bath Scrubber
Loofahs are easily raised from seed. Once dried on the vine, remove and peel off the outer layer. Inside lies a perfect sponge. Remove all the seeds inside and save for next spring's planting. Select a short stick to insert in the loofah as a handle. We like to collect sticks from

the creek that have beaver teeth marks in them. If you don't have access to beaver sticks, then you can wood-burn (burnish) a design, a name, or initials randomly on the stick. Drill a hole in one end of the stick, insert a thin narrow strip of leather, and tie in a knot to form a loop for hanging. Spread waterproof wood glue on the opposite end of the stick and insert up into the sponge several inches. Allow to dry completely before using as a back scrubber in the bath.

❧ *495* ❧

Corn Husks for Autumn Decorating and Children's Teepee

Consider growing some field corn if you have the space and let it dry on the stalk. In the fall make shucks as was customary when fieldwork was done primarily by hand. When cutting the dried stalks, gather together so that the stalks are leaning against each other to form a teepee. Children can use as a reenactment setting of the first Thanksgiving drama. Use excess stalks tied together on the posts of your porch as a seasonal decoration for autumn. Secure to posts with a ribbon and bow. Add a few square bales of hay, some winter squash and pumpkins, and a scarecrow, and you'll make memories that soon won't be forgotten by your guests.

🦋 *496* 🦋

Make your own Scarecrow

If you have a spare bale or two of hay or straw on hand, you can make your own scarecrow. Better yet, host a scarecrow-making party. Invite friends and neighbor children over. Besides the straw or hay, you'll need jeans or overalls and colorful flannel shirts and string. Stuff a shirt full of straw and tie the bottom with string. Stuff the shirt in the overalls or jeans that are full of straw, too. Secure legs and waist with string. For the head, fill a burlap sack with straw and tie shut, or use a gourd or pumpkin. Using water-resistant paint, draw and paint face features on whichever item you select for the head. And don't forget to top with a straw hat to keep the sun off the scarecrow's head.

Cooking Fresh
from the Garden

Gardens and grandparents make great companions. They seem to go together like bees to a flower and puppies to a boy. My grandparents were the first gardeners I knew. Every time our family made the long trip of over 1,000 miles from Florida to Michigan during summer vacation, there were always home-canned jars of Grandma Stafford's bread-and-butter pickles, apple butter, corn, and green beans awaiting us. Although she had eight grown children, there always seemed to be enough produce from her garden to share with us all. Whenever Grandma went out into the garden to work, she wore a wide-brimmed straw hat tied beneath her dainty chin with a long scarflike ribbon. Her complexion was lovely, smooth, and as pale as the moon, so she took great caution to keep herself from getting sunburned. Gardening was one thing that my grandparents did very well together—a time of warm fellowship and closeness shared in the soil.

Grandma died over a decade ago after cancer weakened her. Grandpa moved to a smaller house in town after selling their country house and continued to grow and nurture plants, carrying on what they had started and shared together. Grandpa, alone and capable, raised many vegetables in his kitchen garden and froze many containers of his home-made vegetable soup and chili. When someone came to visit Grandpa they were almost certain to either be served a warm bowl of Grandpa's soup or given some to take home and enjoy later. A jar of his chili even made its way down to me, his oldest granddaughter, here in Tennessee on one occasion. It was like a taste of his home, a way to narrow the hundreds of miles that lie between us. On one occasion, when Grandpa Stafford went for a brief stay in the hospital, he was served soup. Well, Grandpa did not care for the taste. In fact, he was insulted by their attempt at soup making. Being a frank man that always spoke his mind, he proceeded to ask them how they could dare to call this stuff soup! As soon as he was discharged, he promptly retrieved some homemade soup of his own and took it to the hospital. "Now this is soup," he told them. He lived at home alone these past 11 years, gardening and cooking for himself and his guests in this very efficient way, up until his death this past summer at the age of 86. When the contents of his home were divided among the eight children, the jars of soup and chili were considered a welcome part of the inheritance. Now it is left up to this generation to carry on the Stafford gardening tradition of growing, harvesting, providing, cooking, storing, and sharing this rich legacy of garden fresh vegetable soup. DST

✤ 497 ✤

The refreshing tastes from your summer garden can linger long past August when you freeze fresh-chopped watermelon and cantaloupe in Ziploc bags. Great for fruit salad and smoothies.

✤ 498 ✤

Many vegetables grown in the kitchen garden taste great raw. The less cooked, the more nutritious. We should include raw fruits and vegetables in our diet daily. Some vegetables to enjoy raw are young and tender green beans, bean sprouts, broccoli heads, spinach, peas, cauliflower, cabbage, tomatoes, carrots, peppers, onions, cucumbers, radishes, and lettuce. Shred raw squash, sweet potato, and zucchini on fresh garden salads, too. When cooking vegetables, try lightly steaming or stir-frying to retain as many nutrients as possible.

❦ *499* ❦

Bumper crop of zucchini? Cut into bite-sized chunks or grate and add to chili, omelets, or vegetable soup. Shred zucchini with a hand grater or food processor. Put in Ziploc bags and store in the freezer, making it convenient to use for soup and breads. Freeze in the proportions most used.

❦ *500* ❦

Reserve celery leaves for flavoring soups and stew.

❦ *501* ❦

Diced, unpeeled zucchini is good in scrambled eggs. Just brown in a buttered frying pan. Add whipped eggs with a little milk, and when set, sprinkle with cheese and serve immediately.

❧ *502* ☙

Want to make coleslaw, but no cabbage? Try using zuc-chini instead. Shred the zucchini like you would cab-bage and add the remaining ingredients. A similar slaw can also be made with shredded cucumber.

❧ *503* ☙

Cabbage leaves make perfect natural wraps for roasting vegetables on the grill or in the oven. Place fresh veg-etables—zucchini or yellow squash slices, bell peppers, tomatoes, turnip roots, etc.—in the center of cabbage leaves and wrap. Fork through with a toothpick or tie with string and roast for 20 minutes or so until tender.

❧ *504* ❧

Grape leaves, too, can be harvested and used as a wrapper for steam cooking. A favorite filler is ground meat and rice. Grape leaves are also used in specific pickle-making recipes. Schedule pickle-making when cucumbers and grape leaves are mature.

❧ *505* ❧

Corn-canning acid, available from seed catalog companies, helps home-canned sweet corn taste better and last longer.

❧ *506* ❧

Take advantage of a bountiful garden and juice your own vegetable drinks. Live juices are very beneficial to your health. Some vegetables to juice and drink fresh are cucumbers, carrots, celery, tomatoes, and bell peppers.

🦎 *507* 🦎

Okra can be dried easily outdoors on a large screen (window or door) or in a dehydrator or oven at the lowest setting.

🦎 *508* 🦎

After dehydrating okra, convert it into a powder in a blender or coffee grinder. Okra powder can be stored in a jar. Add powdered okra to soups, gumbo, and stew, or use as a binder in corn bread or johnnycakes.

🦋509🦋

When cooking with chilies, scrape out the seeds for a milder taste; leave them in for a hotter flavor.

🦋510🦋

Wear gloves when chopping hot peppers to avoid a burn.

🦋511🦋

If your hands get burned while chopping hot peppers, soak them in milk for relief. Eat too hot a pepper? Drink milk.

❧ *512* ❧

When sweetening cold teas with honey, add honey to a little warm water and stir vigorously to liquefy. Then add to cold tea.

❧ *513* ❧

Eat locally raised honey to build up an immunity to allergies. Never give honey to a child under one year of age.

❧ *514* ❧

For convenience, order empty sealable tea bags from a bulk herb catalog company. Fill with your favorite homegrown dried herb teas and iron closed.

❧ *515* ❧

For reusable tea bags, buy tobacco bags in bulk and fill with your favorite garden herbal teas.

❧ *516* ❧

Tear pieces of fresh, edible flowers and herb leaves to add color, texture, and flavor to salads, dips, spreads, and dessert toppings. Roll cream cheese balls in a mixture of fresh torn pansy and violets, chives, lavender, and rose petals.

❧ *517* ❧

Watercress can be found growing naturally and collected from the shallow water of a creek and used in garden salads. It tastes similar to radishes.

❦ *518* ❦

Peeling tomatoes? Place tomatoes in boiling water for 1 minute, then plunge into a pot of cold water. Skins will slip right off.

❦ *519* ❦

No need to peel tomatoes when making soup base, spaghetti sauce, or salsa. If skins are without blemish, wash and quarter the tomatoes with the skins on and place in blender to liquefy.

❦ *520* ❦

Add salt to vegetables after cooking. It will take less salt to enhance the flavor and salt draws out the natural juices.

❧ *521* ❧

Harvest vegetables close to cooking time or preserve promptly to retain as much nutrients as possible.

❧ *522* ❧

The secret to perfect homemade pickles? Make pickles the same day you pick your cucumbers or at least within 24 hours.

❧ *523* ❧

Potatoes can be prepared with the skins on to offer the most nutrition, even in soups, potato salad, or when mashed. Grate with the skins on for hash browns, omelets, or when adding to casseroles.

⚜ 524 ⚜

When using herbs for flavoring soups and stews, wait until cooking time of food is about done before adding the herbs. This will help retain the full flavor of the herbs. Bay leaves are the exception and should be allowed to simmer in sauces and soups.

⚜ 525 ⚜

Substitute herbs. The herb lovage is a great substitute for celery in soups. Dill can be used in place of salt. Coriander substitutes nicely for cinnamon in desserts.

⚜ 526 ⚜

When making soup, here's some tried and tasty soup blends. Add any one of these combinations to your favorite soup stock.

Cabbage, tomatoes, onions, beans, and corn
Tomatoes, butterbeans, corn, and beans
Beans and butterbeans together
Carrots, onions, beans, corn, and tomatoes

🦋 527 🦋

For a subtler flavor when cooking collards, boil greens with a turkey back, carrots, and onions.

🦋 528 🦋

Liquid Aminos is highly nutritious. A healthier and great-tasting substitute for soy sauce. It enriches the flavor of fresh-cooked greens, steak, rice, salads, stews, soups, stir-fry, salad dressings, oriental cooking, and more.

❧ *529* ❧

Hundreds of other great kitchen helps, cooking tips, and recipes are found in Deborah's book *Pearls of Kitchen Wisdom*.

RECIPES

❧ *530* ❧

Filé
A key ingredient to gumbo.

If you have access to a sassafras tree you can make your own filé. Select unblemished young green leaves from a sassafras tree in early spring. Dry the leaves between two mesh screens outdoors in the sunlight or in a gas oven overnight on a tray with no heat, or in an electric oven at 110°F until dry. When fully dry, the leaves will crumble easily. Crumble the leaves and pound into a powder using a mortar and pestle or grinder. The filé powder will thicken soups or gumbo somewhat. Do not add to the pot until the soup is done. (Filé should never be brought to a boil or it will become stringy.)

⁂ 531 ⁂

Herb Salt or Green Salt
A natural and healthy salt substitute.

Grind equal amounts of garlic powder, onion powder, basil, marjoram, dill, nettles, celery seed, comfrey leaves, and papaya leaves into a powder. Add kelp powder ⅓ total amount of recipe and combine.

From the garden to the kitchen of Vicki West

532

Herbal Seasoning
Good for chicken, pork, and lamb.
 Mix together and store out of direct sunlight:

1 T. oregano flakes
1 T. basil flakes
1 T. sage flakes

533

Herbal Seasoning for Poultry
Mix with a mortar and pestle or grinder and store out
of direct sunlight:

1 t. sage
1 t. thyme
1 T. marjoram
1 T. rosemary
1 T. black pepper
½ t. nutmeg

❦ *534* ❧

Hot-Roasted Chick-pea Tea
Coffee substitute without the acidic side effects of regular coffee.

Roast dried chick-peas in oven until dark brown, being careful not to burn. Grind in coffee grinder.

To make 1 cup of chick-pea tea, bring water to a boil on the stove. Place 1 t. ground-roasted chick-peas into the boiling water. Then simmer the grounds and water together for 7 minutes. Strain and drink while hot.

From the garden to the kitchen of Vicki West

❦ *535* ❧

Basic Cup of Hot Herb Tea
To make a cup of chamomile, thyme, mint, or other herbal tea, follow these directions. Add hot, but not boiling, water to a cup and add 1 to 2 teaspoons of dried loose herbs to a stainless steel tea ball. Cover the cup, allowing it to steep for 4 minutes. Remove the tea ball, sweeten if desired, and enjoy.

536

Fruit Bowl Smoothie

A terrific and tasty way to up your raw fruit intake. This is our Sunday evening special with popcorn.

Yield: 4 1-cup servings

Place the following ingredients in a high-powered blender such as a Vitamix and blend on high until smooth.

1 banana, peeled
1 orange, peeled
2 fresh strawberries, decapped
20 red grapes
3 or 4 chunks yellow or red watermelon, frozen
¼ c. pineapple juice
1 to 2 T. honey
5 ice cubes

Serve immediately.

Note: To use fresh watermelon instead of frozen, add frozen banana and strawberries instead of fresh.

From the orchard to the kitchen of Deborah Tukua

 537

Iced Mint Tea
To make an easy cold mint tea, pick spearmint or peppermint from the herb garden. Rinse under running water and chop leaves well. Place 4 c. of fresh-chopped mint leaves in a gallon jar with 6 to 8 ice cubes and cool water. Chill in the refrigerator at least 20 minutes. Sweeten with liquid stevia or dissolve honey in some very warm water and add to the iced tea. Strengths of various mint varieties will vary. Dilute with water to taste, if needed.

From the garden to the kitchen of Vicki West

538

Herbal Cough Syrup

¼ t. anise seed
¼ t. thyme
2 c. water

Simmer all together for 15 minutes. Add 1 c. of honey and stir to combine. Pour into a jar and store on the pantry shelf.

From the garden to the kitchen of Vicki West

❧ 539 ❧

Horehound Cough Drops
From the herb garden to the home remedy chest.

1 c. boiling water
¾ c. horehound herb, dried
1½ c. honey
⅓ t. cream of tartar

Pour boiling water over horehound, cover, and let steep for 30 minutes. Strain into heavy saucepan, pressing to extract all the liquid. Add the honey and cream of tartar. Stir over low heat until combined. Cook on high, stirring often until it reaches the hard crack stage, when candy thermometer reads 300°F. It is ready when drops form brittle threads when dripped into ice water. Brush marble slab or a cookie sheet with butter or oil.

Pour out the mixture, then score with a sharp knife once it begins to cool. Break into pieces like brittle.

❧ *540* ❧

Lemon-Catnip Herbal Honey
Yield: Approximately 1¾ cups

Gently relaxing, especially nice when swirled into chamomile tea before bed.

¼ c. fresh lemon balm leaves
¼ c. fresh lemon verbena leaves
1 c. fresh catnip leaves and flowers
1 lb. wildflower honey

Grind the three herbs in a food processor or blender until very finely ground but not quite a paste. Heat the honey in a small saucepan over medium heat until liquid, then stir in the herbs. Let mixture cool slightly, then pour into a jar and cover.

Serving Suggestions: Drizzle over muffins and swirl into hot herb tea. Thin with lime, lemon, or orange juice to make a sweet dressing for fruit salads or fresh toast.

❦ *541* ❦

Candied Leaves and Flowers
Borage, mint varieties, violets, pansy, and rose petals crystallize well, yielding beautiful, edible candied embellishments for garden-inspired cakes and baked goods.

1. Gather edible leaves and flowers when dry (after the morning dew has evaporated).
2. Beat raw egg whites.
3. Dip one leaf or one flower at a time into the egg whites.
4. Lay on clean paper and sprinkle to coat with berry sugar (finely granulated sugar).
5. Dry for 24 hours.
6. Dissolve 2 c. of granulated sugar in 1¼ c. water.
7. Heat to 240°F (soft ball stage). Keep syrup well skimmed.
8. Cool slightly.
9. Dip the leaves and flowers in one by one. Or place the flowers and leaves on a rack covered with paper towels. Place the rack on top of a baking tray to catch excess liquid and spoon the syrup over the flowers and leaves. Let sit for 24 hours.

10. Drain on clean paper and sprinkle again with berry sugar. Dry with gentle heat.

✿ *542* ✿

Cayenne Pepper Sauce
Great gift idea.

Fill an attractive sterile bottle with fresh whole cayenne peppers. Using a funnel, pour apple cider vinegar into the bottle over the peppers. Cork or screw on lid and let age.

From the garden to the kitchen of Vicki West

✿ *543* ✿

Pesto
Italian food enhancer and a great way to preserve a prolific patch of basil.

Yield: ½ pint

⅓ c. fresh basil leaves
½ c. olive oil
Pinch of salt
¾ c. Parmesan cheese (optional)
3 cloves garlic
½ c. pine nuts, walnuts or sunflower seeds

Chop basil leaves in a blender or food processor. Add olive oil and garlic and blend for a few seconds. While blending, slowly pour in pine nuts, salt, and cheese and continue blending until the mixture is thick and creamy. Leftover pesto should be refrigerated or frozen.

Serving Suggestion: Mix 2 T. pesto with 1 lb. of cooked pasta. Top each individual serving with an additional spoonful.

From the garden to the kitchen of Vicki West

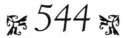

544

Peppy Pepper Jelly
Perfect Party Appetizer
Yield: 9 half-pint jars

6 large green peppers, seeded and chopped
1½ c. apple cider vinegar
5½ c. sugar
½ t. salt
½ t. minced or diced red pepper (confetti)
½ t. minced or diced green, orange, or yellow pepper
  (confetti)
2 pouches liquid pectin
Green food coloring (optional)

Add the six chopped green peppers and the vinegar to a blender and liquefy. Pour into a saucepan. Add the red and green pepper confetti, sugar, and salt. Bring to a boil and add pectin. Boil until thickened when dropped from a spoon (approx. 20 minutes). Pour into half-pint jars and seal.

Serving suggestion: Spread cream cheese on crackers and top with a spoonful of jelly.

🦋 545 🦋

Corncob Jelly
Another great use for corncobs.

12 corncobs
2 qts. water
1¼ oz. powdered pectin
3 c. sugar

Wash corncobs and cut into 4″ lengths. Bring corncobs to a slow boil in a pot covered with water, about 2
qts. for 40 minutes. Strain the corn liquid and measure
out 3 cups. Pour 3 c. corn liquid into a large pot on the
stove. Add the powdered pectin and stir. Bring to a boil.
Then add the sugar and bring to a boil again. Boil for 5
minutes. Skim and pour into clean jelly jars and seal.
For authenticity, add a piece of corncob to each jar before sealing.

From the garden to the kitchen of Vicki West

🦋 *546* 🦋

Mock Pineapple
Yield: 6 to 7 pints
Water Bath Canning Recipe
At last, a sweet way to utilize a bumper crop of
zucchini.

1 46 oz. can unsweetened pineapple juice
3 c. raw sugar
½ c. lemon juice
1 gallon of zucchini, peeled and thinly sliced

Add first 3 ingredients to a large stockpot and stir to combine. Add the zucchini and bring all to a boil. Boil for 3 minutes. Pack into hot pint canning jars. Wipe rims and seal. Process in a boiling water bath for 20 minutes.

Serving Suggestion: Tasty in Pineapple Upside-Down Cake recipe. (see Tip #540)

From the garden to the kitchen of Vicki West

🐦 547 🐦

No-Cook Homemade Catsup
Combine the following and mix well:

6 oz. tomato paste
⅓ c. water
1 T. lemon juice
1 t. molasses or honey

½ t. olive oil
1 t. onion powder
¼ t. garlic powder
½ t. salt

For a thinner consistency, mix in more water. Keep refrigerated and use within a week or freeze.
From the garden to the kitchen of Vicki West

🐉 548 🐉

Elderberry Syrup
Great syrup for pancakes, waffles, and French toast, or as an ice cream topping.
To juice:
Collect fresh elderberries when ripe. (Late August or September, depending on locale.) Roll berries off the branches into a colander and rinse under running water. Place in a pot with enough water to cover the bottom of the pot. Bring to a boil over medium heat. Cook until tender. Stir often. Mash juice from berries in the pot. Strain juice.

To make syrup, add 3½ c. elderberry juice to a pot along with 1⅓ c. honey and stir until dissolved. Slowly stir in 2⅓ c. powdered sugar, adding one-half cup at a time. Stir until dissolved. Continue to cook until thickened. Pour into jars.

Store in the refrigerator or freezer once cooled. Or, to can, seal canning jars with lids and rings and water bath in boiling water for 15 minutes.

From the garden to the kitchen of Deborah Tukua

🌿 549 🌿

Herbed Horseradish Dip
Yield: 1½ c. dip

1 cup fresh parsley leaves, packed
¼ c. fresh chives, chopped
1 c. commercial sour cream
¼ c. mayonnaise
3 T. fresh horseradish, drained and grated
⅛ t. salt
½ t. Worcestershire sauce
Raw vegetable sticks

Chop parsley and chives until fine in blender or food processor. Add the sour cream, mayonnaise, horseradish, and Worcestershire sauce. Process mixture until green flecks of herbs are distributed throughout. Keeps up to 1 week in the refrigerator.

From the garden to the kitchen of Vicki West

🦋 *550* 🦋

Brown Stock
Stock up by canning or freezing this delicious soup stock (base).

Place 6 lbs. lean shinbones and marrowbone in a large stockpot with 4 quarts of water. Bring slowly to a boil. Reduce heat and simmer uncovered about 30 minutes. Skim the fat off the top and add:

8 black peppercorns
6 whole cloves
1 bay leaf
1 t. thyme
3 sprigs parsley
1 large carrot, diced

3 ribs celery, diced
1 c. fresh tomato, chopped
1 onion, diced
1 small white turnip, diced

Bring all to a boil, and then simmer partly covered, at least 6 hours. Strain the stock and cool, uncovered. If there is meat left on the bones, take it off and put it in a bowl separate from the broth. Let the bones cool first. Skim the layer of fat off the top and pour broth into quart jars. Depending on how much meat is on the bones, you can add some to all jars or have some with meat and some clear broth. Wipe the mouth of the jars and seal. If you will be freezing, leave enough space for expansion.

If canning, use 10 lbs. pressure for 90 minutes.

From the garden to the kitchen of Sandra Curle

🦋 *551* 🦋

Miniature Baked Pumpkins
Servings: 1 mini pumpkin per person

A perfect embellishment for roast turkey on the serving platter.

Cut an opening across the top of the tiny pumpkins and scrape out any seeds. Fill hole with a bit of brown sugar or maple syrup, a pat of butter, and a pinch of cinnamon, if desired. Bake pumpkins on a tray at 350°F for 30 minutes or until tender.

From the garden to the kitchen of Vicki West

🦋 552 🦋

Fried Squash Puppies
A delightful combination of bread and squash.

1 c. cornmeal
½ c. flour
½ t. baking powder
½ t. sea salt
½ t. garlic
Pinch of black pepper
1 egg, beaten
¾ c. milk
¼ c. chopped or minced onion
3 c. crooked neck squash
Oil for frying

Grate raw crooked neck squash. Add 3 c. grated squash, the egg, milk, and onion to the dry ingredients, which have been combined. Drop by teaspoonfuls into hot grease. Fry until golden on one side and turn. Drain on paper towels before serving. Serve hot or freeze in Ziploc freezer bags. When freezing, reheat at 350°F.

Frying Tip: Dip spoon in oil to keep batter from sticking to the spoon.

From the garden to the kitchen of Ginger McNeil

❧ 553 ❧

Healthy Baked Sweet Potato Fries
Serves 4
At last, delicious fries without the grease.

1 T. olive oil
½ t. ground cumin
½ t. sea salt
¼ t. Cajun seasoning
2 large sweet potatoes, peeled

Add oil and seasonings to a large bowl and stir to blend. Peel sweet potatoes and half lengthwise. Half again and slice uniformly into long wedges. Toss the potato wedges in the bowl with the seasoned oil mixture until thoroughly coated. Spray a light coat of cooking oil on a baking sheet. Arrange the fries on the baking sheet. Bake on top rack of the oven at 400°F until center of potatoes are done and edges crisp, approximately 30 minutes. Serve hot.

From the garden to the kitchen of Deborah Tukua

Adapted by permission from *Country Living,* a Hearst magazine, Vol. 24, No. 4.

554

Seven-Layer Salad
Attractive salad when displayed in a large, clear, glass footed compote.

1 head lettuce, torn or chopped
½ c. onion, chopped
1 c. celery, chopped
1 small can water chestnuts, sliced

2 c. green peas, fresh or frozen (uncooked)

Layer the above ingredients in the order given.
Stir together topping ingredients in a separate bowl:

2 c. mayonnaise
1 t. honey or 2 t. raw sugar
1 t. seasoning salt
¼ t. garlic powder

Cover salad with the topping and refrigerate overnight. Just before serving, top with ½ to ¾ lb. of fried bacon, crumbled, and 3 or 4 hard-boiled eggs, chopped or thinly sliced. Finish with 1 c. of grated cheese, if desired (optional).

From the garden to the kitchen of Delores Stafford

🦖 555 🦖

Wildflower Salad
Here's a fresh salad to make that is delicate and dainty enough in appearance to serve at your next luncheon (see photo on page 272). My youngest calls these dandy flowers. They make a dandy salad indeed. This

recipe calls for ingredients from nature's garden. We gather these flowering ingredients when strolling down our lane in spring. (Only harvest from areas not chemically sprayed.)

4 parts chickweed
1 part dandelion flowers
1 part wild violets
1 part clover leaves and flowers
tender, wild onion green shoots (optional—use sparingly)

Collect a salad bowl full of fresh chickweed. Gather enough clover, dandelion flowers, and wild violets for a lovely, edible garnish. Rinse all your greens and toss in a salad bowl. Serve fresh with a light salad dressing.

From the garden to the kitchen of Deborah Tukua

556

Raw Vegetable Medley
Fresh vegetables hold the most nutrition; this recipe holds the medal for delivering it with full flavor.

Wash and chop:

1 head of broccoli
½ head cauliflower
1 red onion

Pat dry and place in a large bowl with ½ c. raisins and bacon pieces.

Mix together:

2 T. vinegar
1 T. honey (or 2 T. raw sugar)
1 c. mayonnaise

Add the mixture to the bowl of vegetables and stir to moisten all. Chill several hours before serving.

From the garden to the kitchen of Delores Stafford

557

Deborah's Coleslaw
Yield: 2 cups
Recipe doubles easily. A perfect accompaniment to barbecued meats and fish or seafood entrees.

Combine the following:

2 c. shredded cabbage, firmly packed
1 medium carrot, grated
1 T. sweet onion, grated (optional)
3 T. mayonnaise
1 to 2 T. honey

Note: The amount of honey needed will depend on the sweetness of the onion used. Vidalia works best. If the onion is strong flavored, add 2 T. honey instead of 1. Adjust amounts to your taste.

From the garden to the kitchen of Deborah Tukua

🦜 558 🦜

Potato Salad Southern Stafford Style
This is one of those dishes that I watched my mother make almost weekly as a child. There has been no written recipe for this delicious salad until now. If you serve this with ham or fried chicken and buttermilk biscuits, you've recreated my childhood family Sunday dinners.

Peel 6 medium-sized potatoes, if desired. Or leave the skins on, scrub, and wash well. Chop into chunks and add to a pot with enough water to cover. Boil until tender until they cut easily, but are not mushy. Drain in colander and allow to cool slightly. While potatoes are cooling, add the remaining vegetables to a large serving bowl.

½ c. fresh sweet onion, chopped
1 to 2 fresh tomatoes, chopped
1 c. dill pickles, chopped
1 c. salad olives, halved (with pimento strips, if desired)

Add the boiled potato chunks to the large bowl.

For the dressing: Measure ¾ c. mayonnaise into a measuring cup and grate two hard-boiled eggs into the cup along with ½ t. sea salt and ½ t. prepared mustard. Stir to combine in the measuring cup then add to the large bowl and gently stir. Pour a splash of pickle juice in the bowl and gently stir again. Chill before serving if time permits.

From the garden to the kitchen of Deborah Tukua and Delores Stafford

❧ 559 ❧

Potato Biscuits
A great way to use leftover mashed potatoes.

1½ c. mashed potatoes
2 c. flour
2 t. baking soda
½ t. cream of tartar
¼ t. salt
3 T. canola oil
1½ c. water

Beat mashed potatoes until all lumps are out. Add the remaining ingredients. Mix just until flour disappears. Drop by the spoonful on cookie sheet and bake for 20 minutes in a 450°F oven.

From the garden to the kitchen of Vicki West

❦ 560 ❦

Honey Apricot Bread
Yields 1 loaf

1 c. Grape Nuts® Cereal (may use following recipe)
1 c. dried apricots or raisins
1 c. milk
1¾ c. whole-wheat flour
2½ T. baking powder
½ T. salt
1 c. brown sugar, firmly packed
1 egg, slightly beaten
½ c. honey
¼ c. applesauce
½ c. nuts, chopped, or sunflower seeds (optional)

Heat oven to 350°F. Spray loaf pan with cooking spray. Pour milk over cereal and dried apricots in a bowl and let sit for 5 minutes. Mix flour, baking powder, and salt in a large bowl. Stir in sugar, egg, honey, and applesauce. Then stir in the cereal and milk mixture. Batter will be slightly lumpy. Add nuts, if desired, mix well, and pour into loaf pan. Bake at 350°F oven for 55–60 minutes or until toothpick inserted comes out clean. Cool for 10 minutes before removing from pan. When completely cooled, it may be frozen whole or by the slice to enjoy later, if desired.

From the garden to the kitchen of Donna Prather

❦ *561* ❦

Best Ever Grape Nuts

3½ c. whole-wheat flour
1 c. brown sugar
⅔ t. salt
1 t. baking soda
2 c. milk mixed with 2 T. vinegar (or 2 c. buttermilk)

Mix dry ingredients, then add the milk and vinegar and beat until smooth. Spread onto an oiled cookie sheet. Bake for 15 minutes at 375°F. Remove from oven and allow to cool. Once cool, grind in a good processor. Return to oiled cookie sheet and bake another hour in the oven, turning every 15 minutes or so until crisp.

From the garden to the kitchen of Laine Amavizca

❧ *562* ❧

Pepper Steak with Brown Rice
Yields 6 servings

2 lbs. round steak or venison steak
Buttermilk
Olive or canola oil
1½ c. water
1 beef bouillon cube or equivalent powder
2 cloves garlic
1½ fresh green bell peppers
2 bunches fresh scallions
1 small can sliced mushrooms
Chopped celery to taste (optional)
¼ c. soy sauce or Liquid Aminos
¼ c. water
2 T. cornstarch
2 medium fresh tomatoes, diced
Cooked brown rice or basmati rice

Marinate the meat in buttermilk one hour before cooking preparation begins. Cut steak into thin strips and brown in scant vegetable oil in a cast-iron skillet. In a small pot, heat 1½ c. water, beef bouillon cube, and

the garlic. When warmed, add to the brown meat; heat to boiling. Stir, reduce heat to simmer, and cover. Cook for 30 minutes. Cut the green bell peppers into strips. Dice the scallions and celery. Add the remaining vegetables except the tomatoes to the cooked meat and simmer 5 minutes. Combine the water, soy sauce or Liquid Aminos, and cornstarch, and stir to blend. Pour into the skillet, stirring in, then cover and cook 5 more minutes. Remove the lid and add diced tomatoes. Heat uncovered a few minutes. Serve over a hot bed of brown or basmati rice.

From the garden to the kitchen of Delores Stafford

❧ 563 ❧

Tortellini with Vegetable Medley Cream Sauce
A quick meal made in gourmet fashion.

28 oz. tortellini pasta with cheese filling

In a large pot, bring 4 quarts of water with 2 t. salt to a boil. Add tortellini and return water to a gentle boil, cooking for 15 minutes or according to package directions.

In the last 5 minutes of cooking the pasta, prepare the vegetable medley sauce.

Sauce:

8 oz. butter
1 T. garlic
1 small onion, minced
6 oz. artichoke hearts, marinated and chopped
16 oz. small green peas
1 fresh tomato, chopped
1 medium carrot, grated
Rosemary, dashes to taste
Dash of sea salt
¼ to ½ c. light cream or whole milk
4 t. flour

Melt 1 stick of butter and add the chopped garlic and onion over medium low heat. (Add the marinated liquid from the artichoke hearts, too, if desired.)

In a small bowl, mix the flour and cream together. Pour into the pan with the melted butter and stir in the remaining ingredients except the tomatoes and rosemary. Stir gently and constantly until sauce thickens. Turn off the heat and add the tomato chunks and dashes of rosemary to taste.

Strain tortellini in colander and serve warm with sauce on top.

From the garden to the kitchen of Deborah Tukua

564

Shrimp–Sugar Snap Pea Stir-Fry
Serves 3. A fine dinner ready in minutes.

1½ lb. jumbo shrimp, shelled and deveined
2 to 3 T. olive oil
½ lb. to ¾ lb. sugar snap peas or Chinese pea pods (snow peas), fresh or frozen

Liquid Aminos to taste (soy product available where
  health foods are sold)
Dash of granulated garlic

Once the shrimp have been shelled and deveined,
pour 2–3 tablespoons of olive oil into a wok or iron
skillet, and heat. Add the shrimp and toss over medium
heat. After approximately 2 minutes, toss in the sugar
snap peas and sprinkle a dash or two of granulated gar-

lic. Continue to turn as you cook for a few minutes more. As the oil on the pan's surface disappears, squirt in Liquid Aminos to add flavor and keep shrimp from scorching. Shrimp will turn bright pink when done. Toss in a cup of cooked rice, if desired. Serve immediately while hot.

From the kitchen of Deborah Tukua

🦟 565 🦟

Spaghetti Garden Casserole

8 oz. spaghetti noodles
1 lb. ground meat
1 large onion, chopped
1 large green bell pepper, chopped
1 clove garlic, minced
29 oz. tomatoes, diced
16 oz. cream corn
1 T. sea salt
¼ t. black pepper
2 t. chili powder
1 T. Worcestershire sauce

Cook spaghetti sauce in 4 quarts of water. Add salt.

Brown ground meat and drain. Place in a large baking dish. Add the vegetables, seasonings, and drained spaghetti. Stir to blend well. Cover and bake 1½ hours at 325°F.

From the garden to the kitchen of Elsie Blount

❧ 566 ❧

Cheesy Butter Bean—Tomato Pie
I love this! Onions and tomatoes and cheese are a tasty trio.

Crust:

2 c. flour (1 c. unbleached white, 1 c. whole wheat)
¾ t. sea salt
⅔ c. vegetable shortening
¼ c. ice water
½ c. cheddar cheese, grated finely

In a Tupperware bowl, add flour and salt. Snap on the lid and shake. Add the grated cheese and shake again. Add the vegetable shortening and shake vigorously until shortening particles are the size of peas. Cut any larger pieces of shortening remaining with butter knives. Add ice water and stir until dough is a good consistency to roll out. Line a 13″ × 9″ × 2″ rectangular pan with the crust, reserving enough to form a top crust.

Filling:

1 large onion, diced
¼ c. cooking oil
¼ c. flour
4 cups green butterbeans or baby limas (cooked until almost done and drained)
3 to 4 c. grated cheddar cheese
2 quarts fresh tomatoes, chopped
Sea salt to taste

Directions:

Sauté onions in canola or light olive oil, add flour and stir. Blend in chopped tomatoes and sea salt to taste.

In pan lined with pastry, place a layer of cooked and drained butterbeans; cover with half of the grated cheese. Add half of the tomato and onion mixture on top of the cheese layer. Repeat layers. Top with reserved crust and seal edges with fork tines. Make ample cuts in the top crust for steam to escape. Cook in a 425°F oven for approx. 40 minutes or until crust is golden brown.

From the garden to the kitchen of Eleanor Fewell

❧ *567* ❧

Mock Cherry Pie (Grape Pie) and Grape Juice
Trust me, it's delicious!

Prepare your favorite pastry shell and line a pie plate. To make this pie, you may use either Concord grapes, which are seedless, or Scuppernong Muscadine grapes, which are not. When using the Muscadine varieties, you will need to remove the seeds before adding to the pie shell.

Make grape juice first:

When making from Scuppernong grapes, place them in an open kettle on the stove with some water and cook over low to medium heat until they split open, about an hour. Mash the grapes in the kettle and pour off some of the juice and you've got grape juice. Just add the sweetener of your choice and chill. A large quantity of grape juice can be home-canned. Process in

a boiling water bath canner for 20 minutes for quarts and 15 minutes for pints.

Back to our pie:

Remove any seeds, if necessary. Place enough cups of grapes to fill one pie shell in a bowl and add desired sweetener and dollops of butter and stir to combine. Pour into the pie shell and with pastry dough cut out little circles for the pie topping as shown. Bake until golden brown at 350°F.

From the garden to the kitchen of Kathryn Horst and Deborah Tukua

❧ 568 ❧

Glazed Grape Pie
This recipe utilizes grapes remaining after juicing on the stove. (Read through previous recipe first.)

After the seeds have been removed from enough grapes to fill a pie shell, melt a few tablespoons of butter on the stove and add a cup of grape juice. Add tablespoons of cornstarch until thickened. Toss the split, seedless grapes in a bowl with the juice mixture to combine. Pour into a graham cracker crust or prebaked pie shell. Chill several hours before serving. Garnish with vanilla ice cream or whipped topping when serving, if desired.

From the garden to the kitchen of Deborah Tukua

❧ 569 ❧

Watermelon Sorbet
A cool and refreshing, healthy treat.

Cut one watermelon in half and scoop out the fruit. Save the rind for serving. Place watermelon in an electric juicer or remove the seeds by hand and chop in a blender. Warm the melon juice slightly in a pot on the stove and mix in:

1 c. honey
1 c. raw sugar
2 t. vanilla extract
½ c. apple juice concentrate

Pour into trays and freeze until solid. Cut into strips or chunks and run through a juicer or blender. For serving, shave both bottom halves flat with a knife to serve as bowls. Rub the insides of the rind bowls with honey and fill with melon mixture. (The honey rub will prevent the watermelon sorbet from sticking to the sides of the rind.) Freeze solid again until ready to serve.

From the garden to the kitchen of Adrienne Grass

570

Mock Pineapple Upside-Down Cake

½ stick butter
½ c. brown sugar

1 pint Mock Pineapple, see #546

½ c. blueberries, fresh or frozen

½ c. pecan meal

1 stick butter

1 c. raw sugar

2 large eggs, room temperature

2 t. vanilla extract

1 c. all-purpose, unbleached flour

1 t. baking powder

½ t. sea salt

½ c. vanilla yogurt

In a 9″ iron skillet, melt ½ stick butter and stir in brown sugar. Cover with a layer of the pineapple-zucchini slices, drained (from the Mock-Pineapple recipe, #546). Top with blueberries and sprinkle on the pecan meal.

Melt 1 stick butter and add to mixing bowl with sugar, eggs, and vanilla. Beat at high speed until smooth. Reduce to low speed and add the flour, baking powder, and sea salt.

Mix until combined and scrape the sides of the mixing bowl with a spatula. Add the vanilla yogurt and mix to combine. Pour batter into skillet.

Bake cake in oven at 350°F for 1 hour or until done. Test center with a toothpick. When the cake is done, the toothpick will come out clean. Set a round wire rack on top of the skillet and turn upside down to remove the cake. Allow cooling on rack for 10 minutes; then slide cake carefully using a large spatula or pancake turner onto a cake stand.

From the kitchen to the garden of Deborah Tukua

Index